Risk-adjusted Lending Conditions

Wiley Finance Series

Risk-adjusted Lending Conditions

An Option Pricing Approach

Werner Rosenberger

WILEY

Published 2003 by   John Wiley & Sons Ltd, The Atrium, Southern Gate, Chichester,
West Sussex PO19 8SQ, England

Telephone   (+44) 1243 779777

First edition published in German by Paul Haupt Verlag, Berne, Switzerland in paperback in 2000
Translated by Christopher Massy-Beresford, 4 Vaughan Avenue, London W6 0XS

Email (for orders and customer service enquiries): cs-books@wiley.co.uk
Visit our Home Page on www.wiley.co.uk or www.wiley.com

Other Wiley Editorial Offices

John Wiley & Sons Inc., 111 River Street, Hoboken, NJ 07030, USA

Jossey-Bass, 989 Market Street, San Francisco, CA 94103-1741, USA

Wiley-VCH Verlag GmbH, Pappelallee 3, D-69469 Weinheim, Germany

John Wiley & Sons Australia Ltd, 33 Park Road, Milton, Queensland 4064, Australia

John Wiley & Sons (Asia) Pte Ltd, 2 Clementi Loop #02-01, Jin Xing Distripark, Singapore 129809

John Wiley & Sons Canada Ltd, 22 Worcester Road, Etobicoke, Ontario, Canada M9W 1L1

Wiley also publishes its books in a variety of electronic formats. Some content that appears in print
may not be available in electronic format.

Library of Congress Cataloging-in-Publication Data

Rosenberger, Werner.
    [Risikoadäquate Kreditkonditionen. English]
    Risk-adjusted lending conditions : an option pricing approach / Werner Rosenberger ;
[translated by Christopher Massy-Beresford].
      p. cm. — (Wiley finance series)
    Includes bibliographical references and index.
    ISBN 0-470-84752-2 (alk. paper)
    1. Option (Finance) — Prices — Mathematical models.
    2. Credit — Management — Mathematical models.   3. Risk management — Mathematical
models. I. Title. II. Series.

    HG6024.A3 R67   2002
    332.1′753′0681 — dc21   2002031125

British Library Cataloguing in Publication Data

A catalogue record for this book is available from the British Library

ISBN 0-470-84752-2

Typeset in 10/12pt Times by TechBooks, New Delhi, India

For my family

Contents

Preface 1

It is unusual to tackle a dissertation project 14 years after completing one's studies. In my case it was an assignment at the Swiss Banking School that triggered it off. Professor Dr Ernst Kilgus, who was its Director at the time, encouraged me to develop my assignment, and we agreed in the course of our conversations to bring this about in the form of a dissertation.

At that point I had seriously underestimated the time that would be needed for this undertaking. I had already been a member of Credit Suisse's management team for some years, and was neither able nor willing to work there only part time. So that is the main reason why it has taken five years for this book to emerge. Looking back, however, I can certainly put on record how pleased I am, on the strength of how it has turned out, to have brought this study into being.

I had to reduce the length of the first plan considerably, in order to be able to keep the scope of this dissertation manageable from the view of the reader's time as well as my own. It was originally envisaged that calculations of loan derivatives and assessment of a company's equity would be examined using the methods described here. Although initial results have already been obtained on these subjects, these have had to be left out — but they will form the subject of later publications.

Professor Kilgus said on the basis of our discussion that he was prepared to act as my supervisor for this project. Thanks to his critical observations this book now contains many practical examples and advice to the reader, with the objective of making this work comprehensible and useful to a wider public. I am extremely grateful to my supervisor for his thought-provoking comments, which compelled me to question things again and again. Without him this book would have been substantially more theoretical and thus less easy to read and understand.

On the academic side I also owe many thanks to Professor Diethard Klatte and Rüdiger Frey of the University of Zürich and to Dr Philipp Halbherr of the Cantonal Bank of Zürich. They had declared their willingness to submit my manuscript to critical examination, and provided me with many valuable ideas that have contributed to the success of this study.

I thank my employer, Credit Suisse, for its indulgence in allowing me to attend some of the normal lectures at the University of Zürich during working hours. Included especially in this vote of thanks are many of my colleagues, with whom I was able to have interesting discussions on the subject and who helped in working up the examples.

When it came to this book, I was able to count on the one hand on the considerable support of Mr H. P. Wyssmann, who scoured it with meticulous dependability for mistakes and inaccuracies; and on the other, I managed to enlist the assistance of my brother, Jürg Rosenberger, in its design and layout. Both have my sincere thanks for their invaluable help.

My greatest thanks of all go to my partner Beatrice Wyssmann for the constant exchange of ideas, which covered absolutely every aspect of the work, from the simplest to the most complicated, and for her patience over its five-year gestation. Thanks to her support I was able to bring it to fruition in a calm and orderly atmosphere.

May 2000
Walchwil
Switzerland   Werner R. Rosenberger

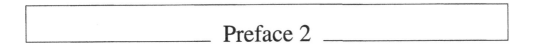

Preface 2

Books about topics in modern finance theory have to be published in English today in order to reach an international audience. This is why I always wanted to publish my book in English too.

I met Sally Smith, Senior Publishing Editor at John Wiley & Sons, at a conference in Geneva in the autumn of 2000. She wanted to publish my book right from the beginning and was of great help to me at all times. I thank her and her successor, Samantha Whittaker, for all the support they provided me.

The next step was to find a translator. Stuart Benzie from McKinsey & Company, with whom I worked on a project in London during that time, helped me to find Christopher Massy-Beresford for this job. I thank Christopher for his excellent work.

My special thanks go to my friend Carolina Schwyn-Villalaz. Her interest and her support have always been very encouraging and helpful.

September 2002
Walchwil
Switzerland

Werner R. Rosenberger

Part I
Outline

Introduction
Rating system

1

Introduction

1.1 THE PROBLEM

A bank can only pursue lending business profitably if all the costs of providing loans can be covered by the income they produce. The bank's income depends on the prices for loans (see Section 1.5) that are charged to its borrowers. It is necessary to know the costs of each loan concerned precisely in order to be able to charge a price that fully covers its costs.

An important element in the costs of making loans arises from the risks that are inseparably bound up with such business. These risks, according to Kilgus [KILG94, S. 66ff], comprise:

- shortfall risks
- market risks
- liquidity risks
- behavioural risks
- operational risks

Kilgus [KILG94, S. 69] asserts that it is absolutely essential that these risks, both in the case of each individual loan and at the level of the bank's operations as a whole, are identified, assessed, controlled and supervised in a comprehensive risk management plan.

It is therefore necessary to be able, among other things, to assess these risks correctly for calculating the cost-covering price of any loan — but achieving this objective is far from simple (cf. [DRZ198]). The necessity, however, also results from the fact, as Berger and DeYoung [BEDE97] succeeded in showing, that a high number of troubled loans brings about a significant deterioration in cost efficiency. The greater the number of troubled loans that have to be managed, the higher the administrative costs owing to increased expenditure on supervision and winding up become (see also Section 1.5: profit contribution rate).

The more precisely the bank knows its risks exposure, the more precisely can it — in the same way as insurance companies (cf. Section 1.3) — set up appropriate precautionary reserves. Unforeseen provisions and write-offs owing to surprise losses on lending business, which inevitably leave the bank's shareholders with a poor impression, can thereby be largely avoided (cf. [SDHJ97].

1.2 NARROWING THE SUBJECT DOWN, SETTING THE OBJECTIVE AND SUBDIVIDING IT

This study will concentrate only on the domestic shortfall risks of any bank lending, in its local currency, to businesses and private individuals, and will not cover lending to the public sector. It will be assumed that the costs of any loan, including the costs that derive from the other risks listed above, are known.

The objective is to develop a model that permits calculation of the lending costs which are caused by the shortfall risk. Following Kilgus [KILG94, S.69] by shortfall risk is meant, in this case, the fact that the borrower is either incapable of meeting, or unwilling to meet, the bank's demands.

To attain this objective, we will fall back on the option-price theory approach of Black and Scholes [BLSC73, S. 637ff]. Our expositions will thus link directly with their explanations (see Section 7.1). These will demonstrate that the Black/Scholes approach can be extended to reach a generalised solution that is applicable in real life.

It is therefore emphasised quite clearly at this point that this study is concerned with developing a mathematical model, which demonstrates the properties specified. As with all models that are intended to be of relevance in practice, it is necessary to compare the model's statements with real life on the basis of empirical testing. Undertaking such empirical testing as well would, however, by far exceed the scope of this study. All that can be done here is to make a qualitative comparison between the results and conclusions of the model, and experience in the lending business generally. This will take place in the context of the examples concerned.

The fundamental basis of the model is put forward in this first chapter. The second chapter will tackle the problem of inaccuracies in the basic data involved, which *a priori* impair the accuracy of the model and make a rating system necessary.

In Chapters 3, 4 and 5 — with the aid of probability calculus — the fundamental correlation between the risk-free rate of interest, the risk-adjusted rate of interest, the probability of bankruptcy, the breakdown distribution probability value, and the probability of shortfall on loan, will all be derived. In the course of this we shall proceed, in Chapter 4, on the unrealistic assumption that the shortfall risk is constant over the lifetime of any loan. This assumption will be dropped in Chapter 5, and it will be shown how the general case of non-constant shortfall risks can be linked up with the conclusions drawn in Chapter 4. We chose this course of action in order to show clearly how the conclusions were drawn. That shortfall risks are not in fact constant over time is demonstrated in Section 7.5 (cf. Figures 7.10 and 7.11).

Chapter 6 gives an indication of how the interrelations derived in the preceding expositions may be applied with the aid of facts determined statistically. But all we will be doing here is mentioning, to complete the picture, the application of statistics as one possible way of solving the problem.

Chapter 7 contains the crucial part of this study. Here we go back to the original idea of Black and Scholes (cf. [BLSC73]) of describing and evaluating debts and equity capital with the aid of their option-price theory. This idea was taken up later by Merten, Geske and others, but never led to completely satisfactory results. The main problem here was that the calculation of the rate of interest consistent with risk was always dependent on the risk-free rate of interest that was consistent with the time-scale. For this reason it has not hitherto been possible to evaluate enterprises with complicated structures on the liabilities side of the balance sheet, as far as risk is concerned, consistently. Thanks to the Nobel Prize won in 1997 by Black, Scholes and Merten this approach is currently undergoing a minor renaissance [ZIMM98]. Related approaches are also being applied to this (cf. for example [GREN96] or [BRVA97]. As already mentioned, these considerations will be further developed here.

The KMV Corporation in San Francisco, California (see [VAS184] and [KAEL98]) is adopting a similar approach. Under this the volatility of a company's value is inferred via the volatility of the stock exchange prices of listed companies. Their model does not, however, use the Black/Scholes equation, but pursues a similar solution approach, likewise proceeding from a stochastic process. In the course of this study, by way of contrast, the volatility of capitalised free cash flows is used to assess the volatility of the company's value using a model similar to the Black/Scholes equation. Loans to companies not listed on stock exchanges may also be assessed using it.

The expositions in Chapter 7 will show that a small detour leads to the objective. The risk-free rate of interest and the rate of interest consistent with risk in the Black/Scholes equation may, with the assistance of the conclusions from Chapters 3, 4 and 5, be suitably replaced by the credit shortfall risk. As a result, for any given company, the credit shortfall risk may be calculated depending on the volatility of the company's market value, on the debt rate in relation to the market value, and on the relevant term of any part of the total liabilities. This calculation may be undertaken separately for any part of the liabilities. On the basis of the various credit shortfall risks, the appropriate loan interest rate consistent with risk can be calculated individually for each part of the liabilities. Here the liabilities side can be as complicated as you like. With the aid of analogous conclusions, loans to private individuals that are consistent with risk may also be calculated.

Chapter 8 will examine how a loan may be calculated on the basis of collateral and how the combination of borrower and collateral that is consistent with risk may be calculated correctly.

Chapter 9 will demonstrate how loans with varied collateral may be combined to bring about debt financing that is optimally structured in relation to risk for any company.

To clarify the expositions so far, Chapter 10 will describe — in the manner of a cookery book — how to proceed in assessing loan risk according to this model. The application of the methods described will be elaborated in Chapter 11, with examples of loan transactions from actual banking practice.

Chapter 12 will demonstrate to what extent the considerations applying to checking loans ought to be adjusted to line up with current normal procedures, i.e., how the empirical test mentioned of the methods presented here may be carried out, and what preconditions any bank would have to fulfil for their introduction.

1.3   THE INSURANCE CONCEPT

Hitherto banks have endeavoured to keep shortfall risks in their lending business as low as possible, with losses on loans being regarded as individual cases, occurring unsystematically, that should be avoided as best as possible. It has therefore to be the aim of every bank, among other things — according to Zellweger [ZELL83, S. 1] — to keep the risks arising in connection with the exercise of individual banking transactions as small as possible. Which risks that result from the business of commercial lending represent the greatest and most commonly occurring ones thus becomes a matter of special importance to any banking institution. Meier [MEIE96, S. 3] also makes it the objective of his work to make a contribution to reducing and limiting shortfall risks.

Traditionally it was the loan official's job to identify problems of customer credit-worthiness in good time, and if necessary to call the loan in. This is always akin to walking a tight-rope, with premature calling in on one side, which has losses of profits on loans and angry customers as consequences, and on the other side calling-in operations that are too late and are associated with the resulting losses in receivables. It is in the very nature of things that any calling in of a loan that is too late is, in every case, seen as failure because of the loss involved. But even in the case of calling in a loan in good time there is always uncertainty as to whether it was really justified in the circumstances. This is extremely unsatisfactory, whichever way you look at it.

We shall therefore adopt a fundamentally different approach here, involving the development not of methods of limitation, but of methods of calculating shortfall risks. Losses on loans will not be considered as individual instances to be avoided, but as costs that are, as they are in the insurance business, calculable. As soon as losses on loans become calculable, it becomes possible to charge an appropriate risk-adjusted price for each loan. It is then up to the borrower to decide whether or not it is willing to pay the price demanded. This way the decision on whether any loan materialises no longer lies with the loan assessment department of the bank, but with the client. The client decides whether or not it is prepared to pay the shortfall risk premium included in the price for the loan.

The task of the bank's loan assessment department therefore becomes fundamentally different. Traditionally it had to decide whether or not the borrower's financial standing was up to the granting of credit at prices that were more or less set in advance. The new task is to charge the right shortfall risk premium for each and every loan, in much the same way as premiums are calculated for insurance policies.

The result of this is that the department of the bank responsible for sales will only close deals in which the borrower concerned is prepared to pay the price demanded. Here it is perfectly legitimate, if applicable in view of the borrower's other banking business, to grant price concessions on loans, as long as the overall relationship with the client is profitable. This does, however, presuppose that skills in the bank's accounting function have been appropriately developed, and that it is in a position to prepare the information that will be needed. It goes without saying that this course of action demands high standards of any bank's sales departments.

As could be seen in the *Neue Zürcher Zeitung* [NZZ96, Nr. 218, S. 29/NZZ96, Nr. 298, S. 19] the then Swiss Bank Corporation and the Credit Suisse Group have changed their working methods for accruing liability reserves profoundly, with loan risks no longer representing extraordinary occurrences, but now being treated as calculable costs. Two major Swiss banks in the lending business have already completed the move over to the insurance concept. According to an article in the *Schweizer Bank* [SCMÜ98] it may also be assumed that the same is now true for the Cantonal Bank of Zürich.

Many banks today have become substantially more circumspect in their lending than they were a few years back, because of high losses on loans in the first half of the 1990s. Now voices can be heard criticising this circumspection and reproaching the banks for exercising excessive prudence. A study from the USA [CPSH98] comes to similar conclusions, in that it establishes that finance companies there may be rather more inclined to take on higher risks, when granting loans, than banks. In contrast to the USA there are, however, no finance companies in Switzerland that would grant loans to companies to any extent worth mentioning. As soon as credit risk costs can be calculated exactly, it will be possible for banks to take on higher risks again 'safely'. It is at any rate important here that the running of higher risks must be associated with higher earnings. According to one study [DICH98] this does not appear to be the case in the USA. A comparable investigation of the situation in Switzerland has not been undertaken.

1.4   TYPES OF PROBLEM IN THE CONTEXT OF LOAN BUSINESS

Our arguments so far rest on the assumption that one has to distinguish, in the lending business, between the following types of problem. It is not absolutely necessary for this that the individual types of problem be dealt with separately by different departments within the bank. It is, however, interesting to note that this is the case among the banks in the Credit Suisse Group. These types of problem are:

At the Individual Transaction Level

- Calculation of the costs of refinancing and underpinning a loan from own resources, including the costs of liquidity and market risks (cf. [KILG94, S. 66ff]): a bank's treasury department usually undertakes this task.
- Calculation of the running costs for the processing of a loan, including the costs of behavioural and operational risks (cf. [KILG94, S. 66ff]: a bank's accounting department usually undertakes this task.
- Calculation of the shortfall risk costs of a loan: this is a question of a new task for the loan assessment departments of banks.
- Negotiation of price with the borrower, taking the overall profitability of the customer into account. The departments of a bank that are responsible for its customers normally undertake this task.
- Handling of delinquent loan business: this task is frequently undertaken by the loan assessment departments of a bank. In the case of the Credit Suisse Group, for instance, there are specialist units within the organisation responsible for this.

At the Overall Banking Level

- Preparation of a management information system for assessing total lendings, and for evaluating the work of the departments of the bank involved in the lending business described above.
- Calculation of the own resources requirement and/or additional liability reserves to cover statistical fluctuations as actual losses appear in any given total lendings situation. This is essentially a question of the calculation of cluster risks and of the effects of diversification.

The tasks at the overall banking level should be assigned to an office that is responsible for the overall supervision and control of total lendings. Banks should be led by the insurance concept in the building up of these organisational structures as well. Any management information system should thus be in the same situation, as is normal in the case of any insurance company, to provide all this information: in other words there is, for example, no fundamental difference between management information systems for an insurance company's motor liability insurance and a bank's mortgage business. Losses calculated in advance according to the model and losses actually incurred must be compared with each other on the basis of various parameters, and the parameters further scrutinised for their relevance.

It would go beyond the remit of this present study to go more closely into the organisation of a management information system and into the calculation of the own resources that would be needed, as already implicitly indicated in Section 1.2, from a business management point of view. At this juncture the intention is simply to point out the need concerned, in order to complete the picture.

1.5   LOAN INTEREST RATE MODEL

The price of a loan is normally expressed in the form of a loan interest rate. Exceptions are, for example, leasing business and consumer credit, the price of which is expressed in the form of regular monthly payments. These regular monthly payments are, however, likewise determined from imputed interest rates. Thus a loan interest rate has to be calculated in the same way as the price for the loan. Our expositions on this are based on the following loan interest rate model (cf. also [SCMÜ98]):

$$i = f + p + r \tag{1.1}$$

$i =$ loan interest rate
$f =$ financing cost rate
$p =$ profit contribution rate
$r =$ shortfall risk hedging rate

Loan Interest Rate

The loan interest rate is defined here as the rate that is charged to the borrower as the price for the loan, and which is indeed paid by the borrower. An integrated loan interest rate is assumed here for the sake of simplicity. Swiss practice also involves charging 'loan commissions' to the borrower in the case of loans on current account. The 'loan commissions' form an element of i, in this model, as the division between the loan interest itself and the bank's commission may in principle be undertaken at will. This simplification may therefore be undertaken for the purposes of the model.

Financing Cost Rate

The financing cost rate is defined here as that rate, the revenue from which will cover the costs of refinancing, of statutory underpinning by own resources, and the costs of market risks and liquidity risks.[1] Here it has been assumed that the bank's treasury can calculate this rate on each loan at a fixed, given level.

These costs accumulate **in proportion to** the amount of loan that is taken up.

---

[1]In Switzerland today uncovered loans to companies have to be underpinned by own resources to an average extent of 8%. That, however, does not mean that 8% of each individual loan has to be underpinned, irrespective of the debtor's financial standing, as is often to be observed in banking practice. It is rather that, in calculations internal to banks, loans to debtors of good financial standing may be underpinned with less of the bank's own resources than loans to debtors of worse financial standing, as long as on average the underpinning is still at least 8%.

Profit Contribution Rate

The profit contribution rate is defined here as the rate that covers the costs of handling the loan, the behavioural risks and the operational risks, and permits an appropriate profit (cf. also Section 4.6) to be earned on the loan. That the behavioural risks are reflected in the profit contribution rate is connected with the following assumptions: normally the borrower is only defined as a behavioural risk if it comes under sustained financial pressure as a result of debt servicing charges. Behavioural risks thus mostly surface only when the borrower has no further borrowing power. This leads to the fact that behavioural risk and shortfall risk are almost identical due to absence of borrowing power. Minor deviations resulting from this assumption, together with the few instances of fraudulent raising of loans, should therefore be ascertained by statistical methods and may consequently be portrayed as part of the profit contribution rate.

We make the assumption here that the office in the bank responsible for sales has to obtain the highest possible loan interest rate in negotiations with the borrower, and therefore the highest possible profit contribution rate: the revenue from the financing cost rate results, after deduction of the above-mentioned costs, which *do not* accumulate *in proportion to* the amount of credit that is taken up, in the earnings from the loan concerned. In this a multi-stage profit contribution rate calculation may be brought to bear. It will be explained in Section 4.6.2 that negative profit contributions and earnings may also result from any loan. We will demonstrate there how the effective profit contribution rate is calculated, if the following variables are quantified — the loan interest rate negotiated with the customer, the financing cost rate and the shortfall risk.

As a more recent study shows [WONG97], there is an optimum interest margin for any risk-averse bank in consideration of credit-worthiness and market risks. This puts a ceiling on any bank's lending activities, in that only those transactions are entered into in which the margin, after deduction of shortfall risk costs, permits a sufficient profit contribution.

In the case of advances made at increased credit-worthiness risk even higher profit contribution rates should be estimated because of the increased administrative expenditure (cf. [BEDE97]). And in the case of advances with higher credit-worthiness risk, increased administrative costs therefore lead also to higher loan interest rates, in addition to increased shortfall risk costs.

Shortfall Risk Hedging Rate

The shortfall risk hedging rate is defined here as whatever cost rate covers the shortfall risk costs of the loan concerned. We assume that this rate is dependent on the financial standing of the borrower.

1.6   MODEL FOR CALCULATING RISK SURCHARGE

In any loan transaction the bank undertakes to pay the loan amount over to the borrower at a defined point in time. In return the borrower undertakes to pay the bank loan interest and repayments on the dates agreed. At first therefore there is a cash flow from the bank to the borrower, and then one or several cash flows from the borrower to the bank. Complicated loan arrangements in respect of amounts paid out and amounts paid back may be broken down into their individual components as such.

Because of the shortfall risk, however, the cash flows nominally agreed in the loan contract do not flow to the bank, but only their probability values which lie, in terms of value figures, between zero and their face value.

Following Volkart's expositions on the assessment of finance contracts [VOLK93, S. 340ff], the sum of the present values of the breakdown values of the cash flows under the loan contract have to be determined, in order to be able to assess the loan that has been paid over. We assume here that the risk rate is correctly calculated, if this total corresponds to the loan paid over. As the correctly calculated breakdown values of the cash flows, which are already an expression of the correctly calculated shortfall risk, may be regarded as implicitly more secure payments, they must be discounted by the corresponding risk-free standard interest rate.

Expressed mathematically, the model for calculating the risk surcharge will now run as follows:

$$L = \sum_{j=1}^{n} \frac{\psi_j \cdot C_j}{(1 + i_s)^j} \qquad (1.2)$$

L = paid out loan amount
n = number of periods of loan maturity
ψ_j = probability of cash flow C_j
C_j = cash flow face value after period j
i_s = risk-free standard interest rate

Here the consideration that it is not just the face values, but the breakdown values of the cash flows that are discounted, is fundamental. The variable ψ_j acquires decisive significance. We will go into this more closely in Chapter 3.

As demonstrated below, the price of the risk-encumbered loan L is expressed in the nominal values of the cash flows C_j.

Continuing, we assume that there is a uniform risk-free standard rate of interest i_s as a reference rate for each loan transaction, which is calculated as follows:

$$i_s = f + p \qquad (1.3)$$

The reason for the standard rate of interest i_s is the following: at a purely theoretical level a borrower might think that it presents no shortfall risk at all for the bank when any loan is granted. There is thus absolutely certainty that the debt servicing will be performed according to contract. The bank only has to charge such a debtor the refinancing costs and an appropriate profit contribution. The rate of shortfall risk is precisely zero. In this exposition the standard rate of interest will therefore take over the function of the risk-free rate of interest in financial market theory, without being identical to it. As will be shown in Section 7.3, this action is permissible as a borrower's shortfall risk, under the theory explained here, is independent of the standard interest rate and of the risk-free interest rate, respectively.

The standard rate of interest does not have to be identical for all borrowers, although it may remain the same for the term. As already mentioned footnote 1, the statutory underpinning by own resources may be varied according to financial standing, providing the statutory requirements are, on average, met. The profit contribution rate does not have to be identical either. Customers of better financial standing usually give rise to less loan assessment expenditure and vice versa, which justifies making such a distinction overall.

Following Brealey and Myers [BRMY96, S. 35] the amount to the right of the equals sign in equation (1.2) may be considered to be the present value adjusted for risk in respect of financial standing, and the credit paid out to the left of the equals sign in equation (1.2) may be considered to be the investment the bank has to make in the loan transaction concerned. The net present value of the loan transaction is therefore [BRMY96, S. 13, S. 35]:

$$NPV_{Credit} = \left(\sum_{j=1}^{n} \frac{\psi_j \cdot C_j}{(1+i_s)^j} \right) - L \qquad (1.4)$$

Using equation (1.4) the requirement for a loan transaction consistent with risk may be formulated as follows: a loan transaction is reckoned to be entirely consistent with risk if its net present value calculated at the standard rate of interest is equal to zero, at which it is the expectation values of the cash flows, not their nominal values, that are discounted.

As the risk-free standard rate of interest in equation (1.3) already contains a profit contribution rate for the bank extending the credit, the appropriate earnings for the bank are therefore built into the calculation.

1.7   ASSUMPTIONS

At this point the assumptions made in this study are listed again:

1. Only the shortfall risk as defined by Kilgus [KILG94, S. 69] is calculated.
2. The price of a loan transaction may be expressed in one integrated loan interest rate that incorporates all the elements of the price.
3. The bank's financing costs and the costs of a loan transaction in relation to market and liquidity risks accrue in proportion to the amount of credit that is taken up, and can therefore be imputed in an integrated financing cost rate for the loan transaction concerned.
4. The costs of processing a loan, the behavioural and operational risks do not arise in proportion to the extent to which the credit is taken up, and have to be imputed into the revenue from, and be covered by, the highest possible profit contribution rate. The revenue from the loan transaction concerned will be calculated via a calculation of profit contribution rate, if applicable calculated at a number of different levels or stages, starting from the profit contribution normally achieved.
5. The shortfall risk hedging rate is dependent on the borrower's financial standing.
6. The shortfall risk hedging rate of a loan will have been correctly pitched, if the total of the expectation values of the cash flows, discounted by the standard rate of interest, are precisely equal to the loan amount extended under the loan agreement.
7. For each loan transaction there is an integrated standard rate of interest as a reference rate.

Assumption 1 is a voluntary restraint for the purposes of this study. It is, however, not thereby implied that no other risks exist (for example, market, liquidity, behavioural and operational risks). The only assumption here is that these risks have already been taken into account (see below).

Assumption 2 is in line with normal banking practice up until now. In the last few years, however, some banks have been attempting to subdivide this principle by introducing fees for administering loans and investigating credit status. Assumption 2 nonetheless implies no qualification to the generality that such fees have traditionally only been applied, as preconditions of the loan, at the time the loan agreement is concluded or the loan is made available. Assumption 2 is valid for the duration of the loan.

Assumptions 3 and 4 are in line with the current practice of any bank in terms of business management. We will not go into the related difficulties in application here, in view of the reservations outlined in Section 1.2.

Assumption 5 is self-evident, and forms the main subject of this study.

Assumption 6 is the fundamental assumption of the model.

Assumption 7 is not made to the absolutely fullest extent for each loan transaction. According to how many lines of credit exist between the borrower and the bank, and to their various time-scales, this assumption may not be completely sustainable. It will nevertheless be made frequently in comparable situations, in order to simplify our considerations (cf. for example [BRMY96, S. 36]. Complicated term structures of standard interest and/or discount rates under equation (1.2) may also be converted to one integrated rate, at least approximately, in the course of calculating the rate of yield to maturity (cf. [BRMY96, S. 646–649]).

1.8 TESTING THE MODEL

A mathematical model is only as good as the extent to which it is able to reflect real life, and this study is no exception. The forecasts made using it have to be capable of being checked against examples of losses on loans that actually occur, in order for it to be possible to make reliable use of this model.

The Basel Committee for bank supervision has tested existing models for measuring lending risks, and has come to the conclusion that there cannot yet be any question of applying such models in the sphere of supervision. Two problem areas in particular led to this conclusion.

Data limitations: banks and researchers alike report data limitations to be a key impediment to the design and implementation of credit risk models. Most credit instruments are not marked to market, and the predictive nature of a credit risk model does not derive from a statistical projection of future prices based on a comprehensive record of historical prices. The scarcity of the data required to estimate credit risk models also stems from the infrequent nature of default events and the longer-term time horizons used in measuring credit risk. Hence in specifying model parameters, credit risk models require the use of simplifying assumptions and proxy data. The relative size of the banking book — and the potential repercussions on bank solvency if modelled credit risk estimates are inaccurate — underscore the need for a better understanding of a model's sensitivity to structural assumptions and parameter estimates. [BCBS99, S. 1]

Model validation: the validation of credit risk models is fundamentally more difficult than the back-testing of market risk models. Where market risk models typically employ a horizon of a few days, credit risk models generally rely on a time frame of one year or more. The longer holding period, coupled with the higher confidence intervals used in credit risk models, presents problems to model-builders in assessing the accuracy of their models. By the same token, a quantitative validation standard similar to that in the Market Risk Amendment would require an impractical number of years of data, spanning multiple credit cycles. [BCBS99, S. 2]

In addition the Basel Committee set out what precautions should be borne in mind when testing models.

The components of model validation can be grouped into four broad categories:

(a) back-testing, or verifying that the *ex-ante* estimation of expected and unexpected losses is consistent with *ex-post* experience;
(b) stress testing, or analysing the results of model output given various economic scenarios;
(c) assessing the sensitivity of credit risk estimates to underlying parameters and assumptions; and
(d) ensuring the existence of independent review and oversight of a model.

At present, few banks possess processes that both span the range of validation efforts listed and address all elements of model uncertainty. This suggests that the area of validation will prove to be a key challenge for banking institutions in the foreseeable future. [BCBS99, S. 50]

In Chapter 12 we will explain what precautions should be borne in mind in order to meet the problems outlined above when applying the model presented here. In this respect it is timely to stress, at this juncture, that methods for testing mathematical models measuring credit risks have still to be developed.

At present, there is no commonly accepted framework for periodically verifying the accuracy of credit risk models; going forward, methods such as sensitivity testing are likely to play an important role in this process. Finally, it is important to note that the internal environment in which a model operates — including the amount of management oversight, the quality of internal controls, the rigour of stress testing, the reporting process and other traditional features of the credit culture — will also continue to play a key part in the evaluation of a bank's risk management framework. [BCBS99, S. 6]

The introduction and above all the regular examination of a mathematical model for measuring credit risks represents a major challenge for any bank, and is at present still closely linked to development of principles. In this respect it is indeed timely to emphasise that the method introduced here may only be examined for its validity in the future, if a bank is indeed prepared to create the necessary preconditions for doing so now.

The Basel Committee made it its primary concern to examine whether there are already models suitable for the purposes of supervision as required by law. This may, however, be more of a second step. Some bank has first to succeed in furnishing proof that it is in a position reliably to measure, and in turn to forecast, its credit risks with a mathematical model. Only then may the extent to which such a model might also be suitable for use for the purposes of supervision, as required by law, be examined.

1.9 LOAN EXPOSURE MODELS

To conclude this introduction, the model developed in this book is set in the context of loan exposure models existing hitherto. To do this we must first briefly review the methods that have been used to date.

The previous models for defining the shortfall risk of a loan can be classified into two groups:

• Classical methods prior to the development of financial theory.
• Methods based on modern financial theory that has been developed since the 1970s.

The previous courses of action — divided into the two groups mentioned — are presented in outline in the following two subsections. The model described in this book is put into context, in relation to the earlier models, in Subsection 1.9.3. At this juncture it is not, however, possible to go all that much into detail, and we accordingly refer the reader to the bibliography. For instance Cossin and Pirotte [COPI01] give a good overall view of credit risk models in existence. The expositions that follow in 1.9.1 and 1.9.2 are based substantially on their compilation.

1.9.1   Classical Methods (see [COPI01, p. 91])

Most of the classical literature on credit risk tends to bear on traditional actuarial methods of credit risk (see [CAOU98] for a survey of these; see also for a critical approach [DUFF95a/b]). Although these methods are widely used in banks, they present some difficulties. The basic principle of this type of approach is to estimate (often independently) the value of the contract at possible default times.

Rating agencies are standard sources for default probabilities. Techniques used to forecast default probabilities for individual firms are described in [ALTM77]. Methodologies have evolved from the calculations of mortality rates to the calculation of rating category migration probabilities. These probabilities (usually organised in so-called transition matrices) consist of the probabilities of downgrade and upgrade by rating category. These calculations are now frequently used by professionals.

As stressed by [DUFF95a], end users tend to develop Monte Carlo simulations without taking into account the uncertainties in the models used to generate the estimates. Second, they rarely take into account the correlations among probabilities of default and estimates of possible losses. These correlations certainly affect the results. One can expect, for example, exposures linked to derivatives to rise with the volatility of the markets. But it is also at such a time that probabilities of default will arise. Unfortunately, historical correlations are difficult to obtain empirically. Some try to overcome this difficulty by using advanced analysis methods such as neural networks (see, for example [TRTU96]).

Nonetheless, all these methods face the major difficulty of being strongly dependent on historical estimates of credit risk dynamics. They are still a useful basis of information to start from, but financial theory has now provided us with more powerful analytical tools.

1.9.2   Modern Credit Risk Analysis Based on Financial Theory (see [COPI01, pp. 9–13])

Modern credit risk analysis, on the other hand, is along the line of the continuous development of financial research on the integration of uncertainty. Broadly speaking, the investor faces risks that are categorised as market risks, credit risk, country risk, and operational risk. Modern appraisal of credit risk follows directly from the advances that have been made for the management of market risks. To understand why the latter has been such a preoccupation in modern finance, let us introduce some chronology about market risks, their development, and the needs that have increased with respect to them.

Market risks integrate interest rate risk, exchange rate risk and stockmarket risk. Interest in market risks began first with the development of stock exchanges and banking systems in most of the developed countries. With the end of the Bretton Wood agreements, exchange rates were then allowed to float causing volatility in interest rates. From the late 1970s, many economic studies were undertaken giving rise to what has been called since, financial theory. On the practitioners' side, many forms of contracts were proposed to the investors to mitigate the increasing volatility on the market, with special clauses allowing them to be optionally protected against changes in the term structure. This produced contracts that not only were sensitive to changes in market factors but also showed discontinuities in them. Therefore, the classical present value of coupon payments and the simple calculation of durations and convexities appeared to be insufficient to monitor and manage those risks.

The interest of academics in developing new theories to modelise the uncertainty of market-risk phenomena has led to a sophisticated set of financial tools inspired from mathematics and physics. The evolution happened on two grounds: financial theory, mostly driven from economics theory at that point; and the inclusion of sophisticated mathematics.

On the financial theory side, most of the research attempted to give a value to the market price of risk or *market risk premia*. 'Market' because the risk comes from market variables and also because, in order to find a unique market risk premium for each factor, the general hypothesis being made is that only systematic risk (the undiversifiable one) is priced.

On the mathematical side, much of today's inheritance comes from the early introduction of stochastic calculus (well known in physics for its application to problems such as health propagation) into modern finance. The contribution of stochastic calculus is firstly its capacity to produce a deterministic solution out of an uncertainty that is modelled as a random process. The dynamics of the unexpected part of the uncertainty is not deterministically specified from the beginning, as is the case with chaos theory. Moreover, stochastic calculus allows the refining of the time space into infinitesimal pionts as a limit of the discrete-time approach. Let us take an example. Suppose that we want to draw the evolution of the stock price and the terminal values that it can take in one month. In discrete time, we have to choose the number of time steps up to the maturity of one month, while in continuous time there is an infinity of time steps guiding the stock price to its terminal value. In the latter case, there are no discontinuities at all in the evolution of the stock price. In continuous time, the process does not execute jumps to two adjacents values but rather changes in a very small period of time to very small different values.

The continuous-time framework is very useful because it enables much more easily closed-form solutions to specific financial problems to be obtained, while the discrete approach is still of great help to visualise the choices to make through time. But these choices are made on specific dates while they are made continuously in continuous time. As noted in Merton's articles, two basic assumptions have to be made to justify the use of continuous-time approaches in the portfolio selection problems of modern finance:

Assumption 1: Capital markets are open at all times meaning that agents can trade continuously.

Assumption 2: The stochastic processes generating the state variables can be described by diffusion processes with continuous sample paths.

The contribution of Merton resides in his capacity, at that time, to relate financial theory and the continuous-time approach introducing the well-known *continuous-time finance*. Before its emergence, financial theory was limited to static theories. Continuous-time finance allowed the restatement of previous problems dynamically, showing how theories such as the CAPM are influenced if the investor is now allowed to behave dynamically. The investor is now allowed to react *continuously* to changes in the environment rebalancing and hedging his positions through time. This ability should be taken into account along with transaction costs to show how strategies can be optimised from the beginning. Moreover, having this possibility means that the investor has a non-executed option on future allocation, which has a price therefore at time 0.

In 1973, Black and Scholes were able to price such complex products as standard call and put options. The contribution of Merton is substantial and visionary, giving rise in the 1980s and 1990s to a rush into the design of derivatives products of increasing complexity. All these tools enable us today to price securities subject to these risks and to design sophisticated contingent claims on the same securities.

Now that market risks seems to be well encompassed, research has turned to credit risk. This interest also fills a need. The wave of developments for market risks has engendered a sudden awareness in other fields, precisely about credit risk, for several reasons. One of them which is very relevant is the fact that differences between European currencies are vanishing with the appearance and global use of the Euro in financial markets. For European currencies' denominated bonds, credit risk then becomes the main determinant of the spread of a corporate bond yield over the risk-free rate. Here, since a linkage is directly being made between the interest rate risk and the credit risk, we cannot stand on traditional actuarial approaches for the credit risk part to price those bonds. Another reason is the huge movements in credit standing characterising the end of 1998. From 1996, we observe a continuously growing number of defaults occuring. With the globalisation wave, falling economies' effects propagate strongly and quickly to high-grade economies. Investors are thus far aware that credit risk is a real problem and that it cannot be measured and monitored on a standalone basis. Therefore, market efficiency demands that the potentiality of credit losses must be accurately estimated and priced.

1.9.3   The Model Presented Here Seen in Relation to Previous Models

The model presented here has two bases. On the one hand it is based on the groundwork developed in Part II of this book on the connections between the shortfall risk of the borrower, the credit shortfall risk, the breakdown distribution rate, the standard rate of interest without taking the credit shortfall risk into account, and the risk-adjusted loan interest rate. These connections are derived with the aid of classical probability calculus. On the other hand it is based on the original Black/Scholes model [BLSC73] for the evaluation of company debts. The combination of these two bases leads to an algorithm that allows the risk of each individual debt position in any company balance sheet to be assessed on the basis of financial theory (or, more precisely, on the basis of option price theory), in line with shortfall risk. This is a substantial advance on the Black and Scholes account [BLSC73]. That an extension of their model is able to achieve such results does, however, also demonstrate how revolutionary their reflections already were.

This algorithm results in one receiving, for each debt position in the company balance sheet, not only the borrower's shortfall risk but also the credit shortfall risk. From these one can calculate, for each position, the probability value — according to the model — of the breakdown distribution rate. Using the standard rate of interest, we arrive at the risk-adjusted loan interest rate.

The great advantage of these detailed results lies in that the fact that they may now be combined with classical ways of looking at things. Let us assume now that the breakdown distribution rate calculated according to the model does not, for instance, agree with previous experience in the case of a concrete loan transaction — or that it has still to be adjusted (cf., for example, Section 7.9). The borrower's shortfall rate determined according to the model may now be combined with the modified breakdown distribution rate, in order to determine the credit shortfall rate more precisely in the case concerned. In so far as it may be necessary to do so, our model thus allows for situations to be examined using a combination of classical methods and methods based on financial theory. When linked in with essential professional experience in lending business operations, it is thus possible to calculate the best possible estimations of loan exposure for given loans (in so far as this is, *ex ante*, possible at all).

The method put forward here is thus indeed based on financial theory, with its associated advantages. Owing to its flexibility, however, it also allows for combination with the results of classical approaches, where this is appropriate and meaningful. In this way the experienced professional obtains an effective instrument for assessing and evaluating loans.

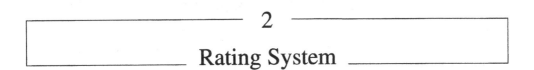

2

Rating System

The necessity for a rating system is explained in Section 2.1, the shortfall risk is defined numerically in Section 2.2, and the credit-worthiness key figure is defined in Section 2.3. A numerical rating system is introduced in Section 2.4 and elaborated in Section 2.5.

2.1 THE NEED FOR A RATING SYSTEM

Kilgus himself emphasises the need to subdivide a bank's borrowers into various risk categories (ratings) [KILG94, S. 70]. We will explain below why this applies here too, and what has to be done to define a borrower's rating mathematically.

The fundamental difficulty in defining a borrower's future shortfall risk consists in putting forward an *ex-ante* forecast on the basis of *ex-post* facts. Historical facts do provide useful indications for this, but the future cannot be considered simply by extrapolating the past. There are, moreover, borrowers that may not yet have any kind of track record. This brief reflection indicates right away that a borrower's future shortfall risk cannot be defined as precisely as one would like, and that a soundly defined estimated value will always be required to a greater or less degree. Anything else would be crystal-ball gazing, as reproducible experiments, such as are possible in the natural sciences, are beyond the scope of the science of business management.

The introduction of a rating system offers a way out of this dilemma (cf. also [CART98]). Borrowers are subdivided into groups with comparable shortfall risks. What this entails precisely is explained in Section 2.4. The individually calculated shortfall risk is not used for calculating the loan price, but the maximum value according to the rating level. The same imputed shortfall risk is therefore allocated to all borrowers with the same rating. This action is based on the realisation outlined above that future values can only be estimated, and that any other action would simply mean faking apparent exactitudes. The use of the maximum value for a group is consistent with the principle of conservatism.

The refinement of the rating system chosen depends essentially on how much cost it is intended to incur on the estimated accuracy of future shortfall risks. This in turn depends on how competitive a bank seeks to be in the market for any particular loan product. The market's sensitivity to price has to be reflected in the rating system. On the other side of the coin, more expenditure on estimation means higher processing costs and with that of necessity a larger profit contribution rate p in the calculation of the price of the loan product.

The question of what might be the optimum estimated accuracy versus the estimated expenditure needed to obtain it can only be answered by staying permanently close to what is going on in the marketplace. There is simply no easy answer to this.

2.2 DEFINING SHORTFALL RISK IN TERMS OF FIGURES

It is assumed here that a shortfall risk ρ in terms of figures can be assigned to each borrower. ρ is therefore defined as the probability that a borrower will, within some future period of time, no longer be in a position fully to meet its commitments to a bank. Unless otherwise specified, we will always be considering a time period of one year. ρ may therefore be assumed to have values within:

$$0 \le \rho \le 1 \tag{2.1}$$

$\rho = $ Shortfall risk

On the other side of the coin, the chance χ may be defined as the chance of any borrower being able to meet its commitments at any time within any future period of time. χ is thus defined as the probability of any borrower being in a position, at any time within any future period of time, of meeting its commitments to the bank in full. Unless otherwise specified, we will always be considering, a time period of one year. χ is therefore assumed to have values between:

$$0 \le \chi \le 1 \tag{2.2}$$

$\chi = $ Survival chance

It is worth noting that ρ and χ are not identical with Ψ_j on the strength of these definitions (see Section 1.6). The correlation between these three values is derived later in this chapter.

Any borrower may be in a position, within the same period of time, either to meet its commitments to the bank in full, or not be in such a position: there is no third option. For any borrower and period of time the following definition therefore holds good:

$$\rho + \chi = 1 \tag{2.3}$$

Bankruptcy cases are far from meaning that all the money lent has been lost to the bank. It may rather be that an expectation of a percentage recovery B may enter into the equation concerned. The following correlation applies, in which i represents the interest that has accumulated:

$$b = \frac{B}{L \cdot (1+i)} \tag{2.4}$$

$B = $ breakdown distribution probability value
$b = $ breakdown distribution rate probability

The breakdown distribution rate is in turn a probability dimension. It is therefore worth:

$$0 \le b \le 1 \tag{2.5}$$

The expectation value of loss in cases of bankruptcy amounts therefore to $(1-b)\,L$. Multiplied by the probability of bankruptcy occurring ρ, the credit shortfall risk ρ^* is as follows:

$$\rho^* = (1-b) \cdot \rho \tag{2.6}$$
$$0 \le \rho^* \le 1 \tag{2.7}$$

$\rho^* = $ Credit shortfall risk

Following on from equation (2.3) the value of χ^* is defined, purely arithmetically, as follows:

$$\chi^* = 1 - \rho^* \tag{2.8}$$

$$0 \leq \chi^* \leq 1 \tag{2.9}$$

χ^* = survival chance regarding the breakdown distribution rate

2.3   DEFINING THE CREDIT-WORTHINESS KEY FIGURE

Under this definition the credit shortfall risk, and with it the financial standing of a borrower, can be expressed in figures by ρ^*, where the value of ρ^* lies between zero and one. As it is normally unwieldy to make a presentation of orders of magnitude using decimal fractions, we make the additional definition here of the credit-worthiness key figure κ as the inverse of ρ^*:

$$\kappa = \frac{1}{\rho^*} \tag{2.10}$$

The following range applies for κ on the basis of the range for ρ^*:

$$1 \leq \kappa \leq \infty \tag{2.11}$$

2.4   EXAMPLE OF A RATING SYSTEM IN TERMS OF FIGURES

The recognised rating agencies subdivide the issuers of loans in such a way that a loan issuer is in principle no different from a borrower. The rating categories are in this sense defined qualitatively as, for example, in the case of Moody's [MOOD90, S. 14/15].

In contrast to this, we are concerned here to capture the shortfall risk of a borrower in terms of a numerical probability. The rating categories in this example are therefore defined numerically. The possible values of $0 \leq \rho^* \leq 1$ are thus assigned to rating categories.

For the purposes of illustration, such a rating system is developed at this point, in line with the following principles (all sorts of other principles could of course be imagined!):

1. 12 levels (AAA, AA, A, BBB, BB, B, CCC, CC, C, DDD, DD, D).
2. As good borrowers in terms of credit-worthiness are substantially more price sensitive than bad ones, level AAA must be selected more narrowly than level AA, and so on: a factor of 2 is used at this point, i.e. level AA is twice as wide as level AAA, and so on.

Supported by the above principles, the following relative widths ensue for the individual levels:

AAA = 1	BBB = 8	CCC = 64	DDD = 512
AA = 2	BB = 16	CC = 128	DD = 1024
A = 4	B = 32	C = 256	D = 2048

The total of these relative widths comes to:

$$\sum_{j=0}^{11} 2^j = 4095 \tag{2.12}$$

The following effective level widths ensue:

AAA $= 1/4095 = 0.0244\%$
AA $= 2/4095 = 0.0488\%$
A $= 4/4095 = 0.0977\%$

BBB $= 0.1954\%$	CCC $= 1.5629\%$	DDD $= 12.5031\%$
BB $= 0.3907\%$	CC $= 3.1258\%$	DD $= 25.0061\%$
B $= 0.7814\%$	C $= 6.2515\%$	D $= 50.0122\%$

and the following applies:

$$\sum_{j=0}^{11} \frac{2^j}{4095} = 1 \tag{2.13}$$

This now results in the numerical rating system shown in Table 2.1.

A simplified rating system for less competitive markets may be drawn up, derived from Table 2.1, with only four levels as shown in Table 2.2.

Table 2.1 Rating system used in the context of this book

Rating	Value of $\rho*$ (%) from	to	$\rho*$ according to rating level (%)	κ according to rating level (rounded)
AAA	0.0000	0.0244	0.0244	4095
AA	0.0244	0.0733	0.0733	1365
A	0.0733	0.1709	0.1709	585
BBB	0.1709	0.3663	0.3663	273
BB	0.3663	0.7570	0.7570	132
B	0.7570	1.5385	1.5385	65
CCC	1.5385	3.1013	3.1013	32
CC	3.1013	6.2271	6.2271	16
C	6.2271	12.4786	12.4786	8
DDD	12.4786	24.9817	24.9817	4
DD	24.9817	49.9878	49.9878	2
D	49.9878	100	100	1

Table 2.2 Simplified rating system

Rating	Value of $\rho*$ (%) from	to	$\rho*$ according to rating level (%)	κ according to rating level (rounded)
A	0.0000	0.1709	0.1709	585
B	0.1709	1.5585	1.5585	65
C	1.5585	6.2271	6.2271	8
D	6.2271	100	100	1

The relative widths of the individual rating levels here come to A = 1, B = 8, C = 64 and D = 512. The factor from level to level thus amounts to $2^3 = 8$, as three times fewer levels occur than in the preceding example.

2.5 AMPLIFICATION OF THE RATING SYSTEM FOR VERY COMPETITIVE MARKETS

The markets for loans to debtors with very high financial standing, above all, are often extremely competitive. The rating system presented in Table 2.1 might therefore be insufficiently precise for such markets. It should therefore be pointed out that the system presented in Table 2.1 may be further refined. There are three times fewer levels in the simplified system in Table 2.2 than in the system in Table 2.1. The relative width of the individual levels therefore grows by a factor of $8 = 2^3$; the exponent 3 being attributable to the number of levels being three times smaller. Analogously, this factor comes to $2^{1/3}$, in the case of a system with three times as many levels, being the third root of 2. By analogy with the method of calculation in the preceding section, one thus obtains the refined rating system shown in Table 2.3 when the number of levels is tripled.

Table 2.3 could be developed over all levels to D. This would, however, be superfluous, as the markets for loans to borrowers of lower financial standing become progressively less competitive.

It must be noted that ρ^* and κ are in each case identical for the AAA, AA, A and BBB ratings in Table 2.2, and for the AAA-, AA-, A- and BBB- ratings in Table 2.3.

Table 2.3 Refined rating system

Rating	Value of ρ^* (%) from	to	ρ^* according to rating level (%)	κ according to rating level (rounded)
AAA+	0.0000	0.0063	0.0063	15755
AAA*	0.0063	0.0143	0.0143	6971
AAA−	0.0143	0.0244	0.0244	4095
AA+	0.0244	0.0371	0.0371	2694
AA*	0.0371	0.0531	0.0531	1883
AA−	0.0531	0.0733	0.0733	1365
A+	0.0733	0.0986	0.0986	1014
A*	0.0986	0.1306	0.1306	765
A−	0.1306	0.1709	0.1709	585
BBB+	0.1709	0.2217	0.2217	451
BBB*	0.2217	0.2857	0.2857	350
BBB−	0.2857	0.3663	0.3663	273

Part II
Mathematical Foundations of the Model

Probability model: Development of ψ_j

Calculation of the shortfall risk hedging rate in the special case of shortfall risks being constant

Calculation of the shortfall risk hedging rate in the general case of variable shortfall risk

Shortfall risk on uncovered loans on the basis of statistics

3
Probability Model: Development of ψ_j

As may be inferred from the basic equation (1.2), determining the probability ψ_j of cash flow C_j being fulfilled is of decisive importance for the model we are describing. The correlation between the shortfall risk ρ and the survival chance χ and of the probability of fulfilment ψ_j will be derived in Section 3.1, with the aid of probability calculus.

In Section 3.2 we will show how the shortfall risk and survival chance might be converted over various terms. Conclusions may be drawn from the results of Section 3.1 for loans that are unlimited in time and for 'reasonable' terms in relation to the shortfall risk ρ. This will be presented in Section 3.3. For the sake of clarity the results of Chapter 3 will be presented again in Section 3.4.

3.1 DETERMINING THE PROBABILITY OF CASH FLOWS BEING FULFILLED

What we are concerned to do below is develop a model for determining probabilities using equation (1.2). The components needed for this model are defined as follows (with the verb 'to default' being used as a synonym for the sentence 'to no longer be able to meet commitments to the bank in full'):

- n is the number of periods in the term of the loan.
- j represents the period concerned: $1 \leq j \leq n$.
- ρ_j is the probability of the borrower defaulting within period j.
- χ_j is the probability of the borrower not defaulting within period j.
- φ_j is the probability of the borrower defaulting between the first period and period j.
- ε_j is the probability of the borrower not defaulting between the first period and period j.
- $\varphi(n)$ is the probability of the borrower defaulting at some point during the term of the loan of n periods.
- $\varepsilon(n)$ is the probability of the borrower not defaulting during the whole of the term of the loan of n periods.

The following correlations apply by definition (see also equation (2.3)) (cf. [BOHL92, S. 312]):

$$\rho_j + \chi_j = 1 \tag{3.1}$$

$$\varphi(n) + \varepsilon(n) = 1 \tag{3.2}$$

The results are derived in Appendix 4. They are:

$$\psi_j = \varepsilon_j = \prod_{k=1}^{j} \chi_k = \prod_{k=1}^{j}(1 - \rho_k) \tag{3.18}$$

In the special case of shortfall risks being constant, the following applies:

$$\psi_j = \chi^j = (1 - \rho)^j \quad \text{if } \chi_1 = \cdots = \chi_n = \chi \tag{3.19}$$

3.2 MATURITY TRANSFORMATION

What we are concerned to prove now is that the values of the probabilities ρ and χ under the above definitions, in relation to the same borrower, are dependent on the length of the period. We will therefore in this section distinguish between the values for ρ and χ in relation to one month (ρ_m, χ_m), one quarter (ρ_q, χ_q), a period of six months (ρ_s, χ_s), and to one year (ρ_y, χ_y).

Let us assume a loan with a term of 12 months. Then the following applies in general, according to equation (3.17) (see Appendix 4):

$$\varphi(12M) = 1 - \prod_{j=1}^{12} \chi_{mj} = 1 - \prod_{j=1}^{12}(1 - \rho_{mj}) \tag{3.20}$$

and in the special case using equation (3.13) (see Appendix 4):

$$\varphi(12M) = 1 - \chi_m^{12} = 1 - (1 - \rho_m)^{12} \quad \text{if } \rho_{m1} = \cdots = \rho_{m12} = \rho_m \tag{3.21}$$

By analogy, the following applies, according to equation (3.14) (see Appendix 4):

$$\varepsilon(12M) = \prod_{j=1}^{12} \chi_{mj} \tag{3.22}$$

and according to equation (3.15) (see Appendix 4) in special cases:

$$\varepsilon(12M) = \chi_m^{12} \quad \text{if } \chi_{m1} = \cdots = \chi_{m12} = \chi_m \tag{3.23}$$

On the basis of the definition, however, $\varphi(12M)$ is the same as φ_y, and $\varepsilon(12M)$ is the same as ε_y.

We can thus now detail the following maturity transformations by using the analogy for the special case $\rho_{m1} = \cdots = \rho_{m12} = \rho_m$ and $\chi_{m1} = \cdots = \chi_{m12} = \chi_m \ldots \ldots$

$$\rho_y = 1 - (1 - \rho_s)^2 = 1 - (1 - \rho_q)^4 = 1 - (1 - \rho_m)^{12} \tag{3.24}$$

$$\rho_s = 1 - \sqrt{1 - \rho_y} = 1 - (1 - \rho_q)^2 = 1 - (1 - \rho_m)^6 \tag{3.25}$$

$$\rho_q = 1 - \sqrt[4]{1 - \rho_y} = 1 - \sqrt{1 - \rho_s} = 1 - (1 - \rho_m)^3 \tag{3.26}$$

$$\rho_m = 1 - \sqrt[12]{1 - \rho_y} = 1 - \sqrt[6]{1 - \rho_s} = 1 - \sqrt[3]{1 - \rho_q} \tag{3.27}$$

$$\chi_y = \chi_s^2 = \chi_q^4 = \chi_m^{12} \tag{3.28}$$

$$\chi_s = \sqrt{\chi_y} = \chi_q^2 = \chi_m^6 \tag{3.29}$$

$$\chi_q = \sqrt[4]{\chi_y} = \sqrt{\chi_s} = \chi_m^3 \tag{3.30}$$

$$\chi_m = \sqrt[12]{\chi_y} = \sqrt[6]{\chi_s} = \sqrt[3]{\chi_q} \tag{3.31}$$

Further maturity transformations may be worked out analogously, under this procedure.

3.3   CONCLUSIONS

Using the special case $\rho_1 = \cdots = \rho_n = \rho$ as an example, some correlations may be shown that ensue as a direct consequence of the properties of geometric series.

3.3.1   The Case of a Loan being Granted Indefinitely

Under Swiss banking practice, current account credit in particular often has no time limit set on it contractually. Equation (3.12) is reformulated as follows for an infinite number of periods:

$$\varphi(\infty) = \sum_{j=1}^{\infty} (1-\rho)^{(j-1)} \cdot \rho = \rho \cdot \sum_{j=1}^{\infty} (1-\rho)^{(j-1)}$$

$$\varphi(\infty) = \rho \cdot \frac{1}{1-(1-\rho)} = \rho \cdot \frac{1}{\rho} = 1 \quad \text{if } \rho > 0! \tag{3.32}$$

Equation (3.32) does, however, only apply for $\rho > 0$, because a zero/zero division otherwise arises. The following applies under equation (3.13) (see Appendix 4) for the case where $\rho = 0$:

$$\varphi(\infty) = 1 - (1-0)^{\infty} = 1 - 1^{\infty} = 0 \quad \text{if } \rho = 0 \tag{3.33}$$

From this one may draw the conclusion that every borrower defaults at some point if the time span for which credit is granted has an infinite number of periods; otherwise its shortfall risk ρ would be precisely zero! From this it follows that every loan must be limited in time, as borrowers with shortfall risks of zero do not exist! In the case of overdraft facilities, this requirement becomes relative, however, as under normal contract clauses notice to terminate the facility may be given at any time. In the course of operational banking this leads to the need to review every loan, from time to time, according to its shortfall risks. If there are changes in the risk position, then appropriate action must be taken: adjustment of the rate of interest, change in the frequency of review, or possible notice.

3.3.2   Reflections on the Success Chance $\varepsilon(n)$

In Figure 3.1 $\varepsilon(n)$ is given for various values of ρ, a logarithmic scale having been selected for the n axis. $n = 1/\rho$ is a characteristic number of periods in this for each curve. It follows from the illustration that all $\varepsilon(1/\rho)$ for $\rho \to 0$ have about the same value. The maximum $\varepsilon(1/\rho)$ for $\rho \to 0$ may be calculated using equation (3.15) as an example (see Appendix 4).

$$\lim_{\rho \to 0} \varepsilon(1/\rho) = \lim_{\rho \to 0} (1-\rho)^{1/\rho} \tag{3.34}$$

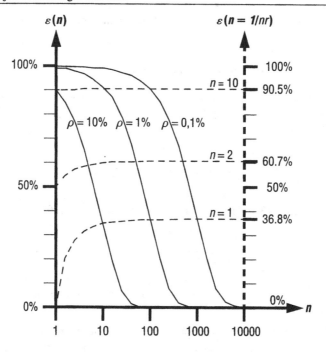

Figure 3.1

The substitution $x = 1/\rho$ leads to [DMK/DPK92, S. 33]

$$\lim_{\rho \to 0} \varepsilon(1/\rho) = \lim_{x \to \infty} \varepsilon(x) = \lim_{x \to \infty} \left(1 - \frac{1}{x}\right)^x = \frac{1}{e}$$

$$\frac{1}{e} \approx 0.368 = 36.8\% \tag{3.35}$$

which means that a loan with term of $1/\rho$ periods has a maximum probability of success of about 36.8%, or conversely, a minimum probability of loss of about 63.2%. It looks better if shorter periods of time related to $n = 1/\rho$ are considered. By introducing the ratio v, the following may be set out, analogously to the above, for $n = 1/(v \cdot \rho)$

$$\lim_{\rho \to 0} \left(\frac{1}{v \cdot \rho}\right) = \lim_{\rho \to 0} (1 - \rho)^{\frac{1}{v \cdot \rho}} = \lim_{x \to \infty} \left(1 - \frac{1}{v \cdot x}\right)^x = \frac{1}{e^v} \tag{3.36}$$

This leads for various values of v to the following values for $\varepsilon(1/(v \cdot \rho))_{\max}$ and $\varphi(1/(v \cdot \rho))_{\min}$:

As may be inferred from Table 3.1, the maximum probability of the success of the loan improves to 90.5% in the case of any term being 10 times as short. Conversely, it reduces to 45 millionths in the case of any term being 10 times as long, or to practically zero! So that the

Table 3.1   Subsection 3.3.2 results

ν	0.1	1	2	10	100	1000
e_{max}	45ppm	36.8%	60.7%	90.5%	99.0%	99.9%
j_{min}	~100%	63.2%	39.3%	9.5%	1.0%	0.1%

shortfall risk of a loan may be kept 'small', the number of periods in the term of the loan must be 'small' in relation to the quotient $1/\rho$.

Seen from the operational banking point of view, this allows us to derive a policy on the intervals of time at which loans should be examined.

It is intended to clarify this by an example: let us assume that the risk of default on a loan should not be greater than 0.1% up to the next loan review. According to Table 3.1 this corresponds to a value of $\nu = 1000$. The shortfall risk might be $\rho = 0.2\%$ per annum. That results in $1/(\nu \cdot \rho) = 0.5$, i.e. this loan must be assessed every six months.

3.4   RESULTS AND CONCLUSIONS

As we have managed to show in Section 3.2, the following correlations exist between the probability ψ_j, the shortfall risk ρ and the survival chance χ:

$$\psi_j = \varepsilon_j = \prod_{k=1}^{j} \chi_k = \prod_{k=1}^{j} (1 - \rho_k) \tag{3.18}$$

and, respectively:

$$\psi_j = \chi^j = (1 - \rho)^j \quad \text{if } \chi_1 = \cdots = \chi_n = \chi \tag{3.19}$$

In the event that the shortfall risk ρ or the survival chance χ are known for a specified period of time, then the values for t periods may be calculated as follows; t may be assumed to have all values between zero and infinity:

$$\rho(t) = 1 - (1 - \rho)^t \tag{3.24}$$

$$\chi(t) = \chi^t \tag{3.28}$$

Under the conclusions of Section 3.3, all loans should be limited in time or provided with a contractual clause providing for unilateral termination. This follows from the fact that any loan with an infinite term will, in accordance with practical considerations, default at some point in time. The maximum term must be selected in proportion to the quotient $1/\rho$. A bank's lending policy will find its expression in the value ascribed to this factor. The methods of calculation outlined in Table 3.1 and in turn in subsection 3.3.2 form the necessary aids to decision making in this respect.

4

Calculation of the Shortfall Risk Hedging Rate in the Special Case of Shortfall Risks being Constant

This chapter is concerned with calculating the shortfall risk hedging rate ρ for different types of loan, using equations (1.2), (2.4) and (3.19), considering for the time being just the special case $\rho_1 = \cdots = \rho_n = \rho$ over the entirety of n periods of the loan term.

It is completely clear that the assumption of the shortfall risk ρ being constant over the entire term of any loan is unrealistic. This assumption will be dropped in Chapter 5, and we will show how the general case of shortfall risks being non-constant may be combined with the results of Chapter 4. This course of action was chosen in order to make the derivation of the results more open. That shortfall risks are not in fact constant over time will be shown in Section 7.5 (cf. Figures 7.10 and 7.11).

Sections 4.1 and 4.6 are central to this chapter. The correlation between the shortfall risk hedging rate r, the breakdown distribution rate probability b, the shortfall risk ρ and the risk exposure ρ^* will be derived in Section 4.1. We will show in Sections 4.2 to 4.4 that all known forms of clean credit may be described substantially with the same equations as in Section 4.1, and that assessment of loans follows the same rules.

Based on Section 4.1, some operational conclusions are derived in Section 4.6. Section 4.7 summarises the most important results again, and these are illustrated in Section 4.8 by means of an example.

4.1 FIXED ADVANCE WITHOUT REPAYMENTS

Loans of this kind take the form, at first, of a cash flow from the bank to the borrower, i.e. the total of the loan is paid out. There then follow several cash flows from the borrower to the bank, covering the regular interest payments and the repayment of the loan at the end of the term. In the event that the borrower defaults, the breakdown distributions concerned take the place of repayment. If the loan is covered, the equivalent values should count as being included in the collateral.

The following thus applies, according to equations (1.2), (2.4) and (3.19):

$$\Lambda = \left(\sum_{j=1}^{n} \frac{\chi^j \cdot i \cdot L}{(1+i_s)^j} \right) + \frac{\chi^n \cdot L}{(1+i_s)^n} + \left(\sum_{j=1}^{n} \frac{\chi^{j-1} \cdot \rho \cdot b \cdot L \cdot (1+i)}{(1+i_s)^j} \right) \tag{4.1}$$

Λ : loan market value

L represents the amount of loan paid out. The first summand (in the first set of brackets) represents the sum of the discounted expectation values of the interest payments. The second summand represents the expectation value of the discounted loan repayment.

The third summand (in the second set of brackets) represents the sum of the expectation values of the breakdown distributions for each individual period. Here it has been assumed that the breakdown distributions will be paid out at the end of the period in which the borrower defaulted and will always be of the same size, irrespective of the period concerned. The factor χ^{j-1} represents the probability that default on the loan will not have occurred in the first $j - 1$ periods.

The factor ρ represents the probability that default on the loan does occur in period j. $L(1 + i)$ represents the lender's demands, where for the sake of simplicity it is assumed that the full amount of interest for the period j will become due in the case of bankruptcy. It is thus being assumed, for the sake of simplicity and without departing much from real-life circumstances, that if bankruptcy occurs at all it occurs precisely at the end of the period concerned. Under our assumptions interest was in practice paid during the first $j - 1$ periods.

Comparison with the study of Fooladi, Roberts and Skimmer is interesting at this juncture. Their thesis is indeed the duration of obligations in cases where credit-worthiness is at risk [FRSK97]; they did, however, also have to establish a correlation between loan interest, risk-free interest and shortfall risk. Their starting equation is therefore very similar. They do, however, deal with the general case right from the beginning (see later in Chapter 5).

When a loan is paid out, its market value must correspond at least to its nominal value: $\Lambda \geq L$. The bank would otherwise be already accepting a loss at that point. In what follows it is intended that r is calculated in such a way that the market value and nominal value of the loan are identical when it is paid out: $\Lambda = L$ (cf. Section 1.6).

The result reads as follows (see Appendix 5 for derivation):

$$r = \frac{\rho^*}{1 - \rho^*} \cdot (1 + i_s) \tag{4.14}$$

In this way the final result for the shortfall risk hedging rate r is, following from the assumption that shortfall risks are constant, independent of the number of periods in the term of the loan!

This comes about because the revenue arising from the shortfall risk hedging rate in the case of interest being paid in each period precisely covers the rise in the shortfall risk of the loan repayment. Seen mathematically, it is a consequence of the properties of geometrical series.

The correlation between r, i_s, and ρ^* and b is portrayed graphically in Figures 4.1 and 4.2.

The higher the risk-free rate of interest i_s, the higher will also be the risk premium r in the case of the same credit shortfall risk ρ^*, as interest payments do indeed also have to be 'insured' from the point of view of risk.

If a 100% breakdown distribution were assumed in an extreme case, then the risk of default on the loan would be zero, and with it the risk premium too.

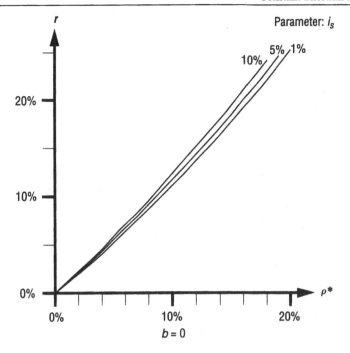

Figure 4.1

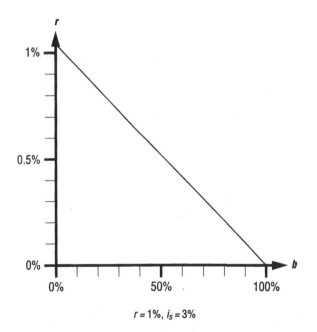

Figure 4.2

4.2   FIXED ADVANCE WITH REGULAR REPAYMENTS

This type of loan relies on fixed advance disbursement without repayments, in that each individual repayment tranche is regarded as an independent loan in the form of a fixed advance disbursement, without repayments. Equation (4.14) applies again to these individual loans. The same shortfall risk hedging rate results for all the part loans, on account of their independence from the number of periods in the term of the loan, and therefore for the loan as a whole too.

4.3   LOANS ON REGULAR ANNUAL REPAYMENT

In Swiss banking practice, consumer credit and leasing credit is mainly granted in the form of loans on regular annual repayment. The borrower or lessee thus makes regular fixed payments (for example monthly, quarterly or every six months) to the lender or lessor, as the case may be. The amount includes both interest and repayment. As the amount is fixed, it contains a high proportion of interest and a low proportion of repayment at the beginning of the term. Towards the end of the term it is exactly the other way round, as the proportion of interest in the total annual payment becomes smaller and smaller owing to the repayments accumulating (cf. [BRMY96, S. 39–41].

The same considerations apply analogously to this type of credit as to fixed advance with regular repayments. The only difference between these two types of credit lies in the fact that the sizes of the 'imagined' part loans vary considerably. This does not, however, alter the validity of equation (4.14).

4.4   CURRENT ACCOUNT CREDIT

In the case of current account credit, the bank agrees a maximum credit limit with the borrower. In contrast to fixed advance credit this gives the borrower leeway to decide each day how much credit to take up, as he draws money in or pays it out. Loan interest is only calculated on the amount of credit actually utilised each day.

The following problems for the bank in respect of the three elements that make up the loan interest rate (see equation (1.1)) arise from this.

Financing Rate f

No problems arise here if we make the assumption that only those costs which are incurred in proportion to the amount of credit taken up are built into the financing rate f.

Profit Contribution Rate p

Granting and supervising current account credit creates costs for the bank which are incurred anyway, whether or not the credit is then taken up. The best case for the bank is the permanent and full utilisation of the credit, as this allows the highest amounts of interest, and thus the highest contributions to the covering of costs, to be billed. The worst case is, vice versa, when the credit is granted but not utilised, as in this case there are indeed costs, but no service is provided that can be billed. In accordance with Section 1.2, however, it is not our intention to go into this problem more closely here.

Shortfall Risk Hedging Rate r

The situation here is similar to the profit contribution rate. Revenue from the shortfall risk hedging rate only arises if the credit is taken up. Vice versa, however, risk for the bank only arises for the bank if it is taken up and only to the extent that it is utilised. So no problem arises as long as the average utilisation of the loan prior to default on it is the same as the extent to which the credit is taken up at the time of the default.

Banking practice does, however, paint a different picture. Experience shows that current account credit is fully utilised at the time of default, and from time to time is even actually exceeded. On the other hand, by virtue of the very nature of current account credit, utilisation is by no means always necessarily full prior to default. Even borrowers who do not default do not always use their credit limit absolutely fully and thus never pay, in relation to the limit granted (which corresponds *de facto* to the bank's effective lending risk), a full risk premium.

The circumstances outlined have the effect that equation (4.14) may not be applied across the board in the case of current account credit. The overall necessary return from the shortfall risk hedging rate R_n across a bank's entire current account credit portfolio of m individual credit arrangements is calculated by the summation of all m individual loans at the shortfall risk hedging rate ρ_j^* concerned, according to equation (4.14), multiplied by the loan granted in each case L_g (see Appendix 5 for derivation):

$$R_n = \sum_{j=1}^{m} \frac{\rho^* j}{1 - \rho^* j} \cdot (1 + i_{sj}) \cdot L_{gj} \tag{4.19}$$

R_n = necessary return
L_g = granted loan

But only the current account credit write-off risk hedging rate r_{cacj}, agreed with the customer, multiplied by the average amounts of credit taken up in each case L_u, may be billed:

$$R_b = \sum_{j=1}^{n} r_{cacj} \cdot L_{uj} \tag{4.20}$$

R_b = billed return
r_{cac} = current account credit write-off risk hedging rate
L_u = used loan

The simplest solution for bridging this difference consists in demanding an arrangement fee for each current account credit, whether or not the credit is taken up. The size of this arrangement fee corresponds here to the shortfall risk hedging rate under equation (4.14), multiplied by the loan granted. Traditionally the Swiss lending market has, however, not permitted this way of proceeding, which is why the solution given below has been developed.

It is intended to assume in what follows, for the sake of simplicity, that in the case of current account borrowers the bank multiplies the risk rate under equation (4.14) for all borrowers by a correction factor r_c:

$$r_{cacj} = r_c \cdot \frac{\rho_j^*}{1 - \rho_j^*} \cdot (1 + i_{sj}) \tag{4.21}$$

$r_c =$ correction factor

Using this correction factor, the intention is to achieve a position in which the risk premium that is necessary and the risk premium that has been billed are identical.

The following equation for determining r_c may now be drawn up, with the aid of equations (4.19), (4.20) and (4.21):

$$\sum_{j=1}^{m} \frac{\rho_j^*}{1 - \rho_j^*} \cdot (1 + i_s) \cdot L_{gj} = \sum_{j=1}^{m} r_c \cdot \frac{\rho_j^*}{1 - \rho_j^*} \cdot (1 + i_s) \cdot L_{uj} \tag{4.22}$$

As the correction factor is a constant, it can be placed in front of the sum. Subsequent division gives the following result for r_c:

$$r_c = \frac{\sum_{j=1}^{m} \frac{\rho_j^*}{1-\rho_j^*} \cdot (1 + i_s) \cdot L_{gj}}{\sum_{j=1}^{m} \frac{\rho_j^*}{1-\rho_j^*} \cdot (1 + i_s) \cdot L_{uj}} \tag{4.23}$$

In relation to the past, the resulting calculation can be undertaken without further ado, though only with considerable computation. The calculation of r_c for future periods is, however, more problematic, as in this case the amounts of credit utilised L_{uj} have to be estimated for the future. In times of rapid economic change this might only be possible very imprecisely.

Introducing a rating system, as explained in Chapter 2, allows us to come to grips with this difficulty more successfully. The imputed ρ_k^* for all loans within a defined rating level k are identical and therefore constant. The figures may therefore be taken out of their brackets as follows:

$$r_{ck} = \frac{\frac{\rho_j^*}{1-\rho_j^*} \cdot (1 + i_s) \cdot \sum_{j=1}^{m_k} L_{gkj}}{\frac{\rho_j^*}{1-\rho_j^*} \cdot (1 + i_s) \cdot \sum_{j=1}^{m_k} L_{ukj}} \tag{4.24}$$

which is reduced to:

$$r_{ck} = \frac{\sum_{j=1}^{m_k} L_{gkj}}{\sum_{j=1}^{m_k} L_{ukj}} \tag{4.25}$$

The risk premium rate r_{cack} for any current account credit at the rating level k with m_k individual loans and the credit shortfall risks therefore associated with them of ρ_k^* is thus calculated in the following way:

$$r_{cack} = \frac{\sum\limits_{j=1}^{m_k} L_{gkj}}{\sum\limits_{j=1}^{m_k} L_{ukj}} \cdot \frac{\rho_j^*}{1 - \rho_j^*} \cdot (1 + i_s) \tag{4.26}$$

The values for the future periods to be calculated must be inserted in the case of both totals in equation (4.26). In practice it remains to be investigated whether the future values may be approximated sufficiently precisely by reference to past values, or whether a special procedure has to be developed.

High unutilised current account credit limits lead to high rates of interest on current accounts, because of the quotient of the two totals in equation (4.26). This results in so-called 'inventory limits' (i.e. longer term unutilised current account credit limits) inevitably raising the level of current account interest rates. 'Inventory limits' are thus to be avoided, if possible, in the context of being competitive as far as interest rates are concerned. For the borrower this means that it should be budgeting its future credit needs as precisely as possible and applying to its bank for an appropriate credit limit. The more accurately it is in a position to budget, the less need it has to bring imponderables into its considerations. This has the consequence that borrowers should not apply to banks for unnecessarily high credit limits just because, for example, a competitor has a similar credit limit at its disposal, or because the borrower wishes to make capital out of the size of its credit limit.

The problem of 'inventory limits' is at its most conspicuous with construction loans. By their very nature these are only utilised fully at the end of the term, i.e. prior to consolidation. If a construction loan deteriorates from the point of view of credit-worthiness during the construction period — whether it be owing to the client's financial standing or to the quality of the construction project in hand — it is usually pointless for the bank to call in the loan, as during the term of such a loan there is only an unfinished building to show for it. In this situation the bank has no alternative but to complete the building at its own expense and therefore in practice, *de facto*, to pay the loan off. As invoices for works completed are in each case settled as late as possible, the extent to which any construction loan is taken up is equivalent to an average utilisation of about one-third. Under equation (4.26) this leads to a shortfall risk charge three times higher than that for full utilisation. We permit ourselves at this point the conjecture that construction loans, seen in isolation, have historically been under-priced. Attractively priced construction loans may, however, be a means of canvassing new mortgage business, and therefore be justified on marketing grounds, but this presupposes a matching degree of customer loyalty.

As already mentioned the problem of only partial utilisation, particularly in the case of current account loans, may also be solved by arrangement fees on credit limits *granted*. This would also be a solution in relation to the billing of profit contributions that might not otherwise be obtained. Furthermore the difficulty of 'inventory limits' could be effectively countered, as presumably only a very few borrowers are prepared to pay an arrangement fee for a credit limit that may hardly ever be utilised. If the price elements p and r (see equation (1.1)) are billed in the form of an arrangement fee, then on the other hand it is still only the price element f that rises in proportion to the loan being taken up. In practice this may, for example, lead to a current account credit priced today with interest at 5% per annum and with a fee of 0.25% per quarter being demanded, being charged in future at 4% per annum on the amount of loan actually taken up and at a fee of 0.5% per quarter on the amount of credit *granted*. Such an arrangement fee should not, however, be forced upon the Swiss market for credit at the moment.

If cases of exceeding limits are ignored, it may be said that the following always applies:

$$L_{uk} < L_{gk} \qquad (4.27)$$

From this it may be concluded that the following always applies:

$$r_{ck} > 1 \qquad (4.28)$$

This allows us to note, purely qualitatively, that any current account credit facility for the same borrower is always associated with a higher loan interest rate than fixed advance credit, providing the risk-free rate of interest i_s is identical in both cases. But even if i_s is not identical, then it may be emphasised that current account credit must, on the strength of the expositions in this section, tend to be more expensive than fixed advance credit.

So a lending policy could consist in only granting fixed advances that are *fully utilised at any one time* and operating current accounts only on the basis of credit balances. The advantage of being able to give immediate notice on current account facilities in cases indicating that those facilities should be withdrawn is in many cases illusory anyway. Moreover the qualifying time until maturity in the case of fixed advances, of three or six months, would not be excessively long. If winding up such advances does occur, one may always fall back on current account lending. This is no arithmetical problem here, as experience shows that current account credit facilities are fully utilised in such situations and therefore are tantamount to *de facto* fixed advances.

One further problem in current account lending is the tiresome subject of current account facilities being exceeded. The most effective method of meeting this difficulty is the charging of fees or of a special rate of interest on the excess, which would cover the additional risks even in the most unfavourable instance. As the allowing of credit to be exceeded means a great and in no way automatic concession by the bank, matching prices may also be applied here. The exceeding of credit limits is, however, usually also an indication of deteriorating credit-worthiness on the part of the borrower, and calls therefore for reassessment of the lending. Here it must also be established, in particular, whether or not the high loan interest rates associated with the excess borrowing can be borne by the borrower: over-mechanical applications of higher rates of interest may cause additional credit-worthiness problems and thereby become self-fulfilling prophecies. If credit limits are exceeded over a longer period of time, a decision must be taken as to whether the normal credit limit could be raised, or whether it is a case for withdrawal of credit.

4.5   LOAN ASSESSMENT

This chapter has so far shown how the shortfall risk hedging rate r should be calculated when paying out a loan. Any borrower's credit-worthiness may, however, change during the term of a loan. By applying equation (4.1) the market value of a loan L_l for the last l periods of the term can be detailed as follows:

$$\Lambda_l = \left(\sum_{j=1}^{l} \frac{\chi_l^j \cdot i \cdot L}{(1 + i_{sl})^j} \right) + \frac{L}{(1 + i_{sl})^l} + \left(\sum_{j=1}^{l} \frac{\chi_l^{j-1} \cdot \rho_l \cdot b \cdot L \cdot (1 + i)}{(1 + i_{sl})^j} \right) \quad (4.29)$$

The value of i_{sl} at the time of the assessment does not necessarily have to coincide with the value of i_s at the time of paying out the loan, which is expressed by the index I.

The equation factor λ for correcting the assessment of market value in relation to nominal value is derived in Appendix 5.

$$\lambda = \frac{\left((1 + i_{sl})^l - \chi_l^l\right) \cdot ((1 + i) \cdot (\rho_l \cdot b + \chi_l) - i_{sl} - 1)}{(1 + i_{sl})^l \cdot (1 + i_{sl} - \chi_l)} \quad (4.38)$$

The left-hand bracket in the numerator and the denominator in equation (4.38) are always positive because of the definitions of the values occurring. An appreciation profit thus exists if the right-hand bracket in the numerator of equation (4.38) is positive. If it is negative, circumstances have arisen requiring a provision to be made:

$$(1 + i) \cdot (\rho_l \cdot b + \chi_l) > 1 + i_{sl} \Rightarrow \text{appreciation profit}$$
$$(1 + i) \cdot (\rho_l \cdot b + \chi_l) < 1 + i_{sl} \Rightarrow \text{requiring a provision} \quad (4.39)$$

No assessment correction is necessary if this bracket is equivalent to zero, i.e.

$$(1 + i) \cdot (\rho_l \cdot b + \chi_l) = 1 + i_{sl} \quad (4.40)$$

$$(1 + i) = \frac{1 + i_{sl}}{\rho_l \cdot b + 1 - \rho_l} \quad (4.41)$$

$$i = \frac{1 + i_{sl}}{1 - \rho_l \cdot (1 - b)} - 1 \quad (4.42)$$

$$i = \frac{1 + i_{sl} - 1 + \rho_l \cdot (1 - b)}{1 - \rho_l \cdot (1 - b)} \quad (4.43)$$

$$i = \frac{i_{sl} + \rho_l \cdot (1 - b)}{1 - \rho_l \cdot (1 - b)} \quad (4.44)$$

$$i = \frac{i_{sl} + \rho_l^*}{1 - \rho_l^*} = i_l \quad (4.45)$$

Equation (4.45) is identical to equation (4.49) (see Section 4.6). There is thus no need for assessment correction if the risk-adjusted rate of interest $i_l l$ periods prior to the end of the term is identical to the risk-adjusted rate of interest when the loan is paid out!

4.6 CONCLUSIONS

The following conclusions can be drawn by derivation from equation (4.14).

4.6.1   Minimum Loan Interest Rate

Equations (1.3) and (4.14) inserted into equation (1.1) will yield:

$$i = i_s + \frac{\rho^*}{1 - \rho^*} \cdot (1 + i_s) \tag{4.46}$$

Equation (4.46) can be simplified as follows:

$$i = \frac{i_s \cdot (1 - \rho^*) + \rho^* \cdot (1 + i_s)}{1 - \rho^*} \tag{4.47}$$

$$i = \frac{i_s - i_s \cdot \rho^* + \rho^* + i_s \cdot \rho^*}{1 - \rho^*} \tag{4.48}$$

$$i = \frac{i_s + \rho^*}{1 - \rho^*} \tag{4.49}$$

The loan interest rate under equation (4.49) can now be interpreted in the case of the minimum rate of interest given i_{smin} or risk-free loans and the credit shortfall risk given ρ^* as minimum rate of interest i_{min}, and it is this loan interest rate that must be billed to the customer in order to achieve the necessary minimum profit contribution:

$$i_{min} = \frac{i_{smin} + \rho^*}{1 - \rho^*} = \frac{f + p_{min} + \rho^*}{1 - \rho^*} \tag{4.50}$$

See Figure 4.3 for illustration of the correlations.

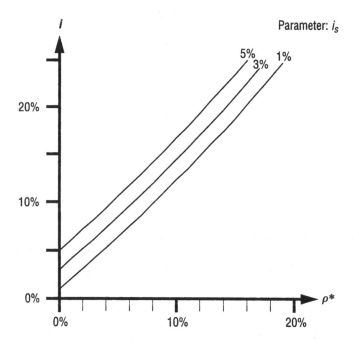

Figure 4.3

4.6.2 Effective Profit Contribution Rate

The bank will in practice agree with the customer an effective loan interest rate i_{eff}, which is not necessarily identical to the minimum loan interest rate i_{min} according to equation (4.50). This leads to an effective profit contribution rate p_{eff}, which is thus not identical to the minimum profit contribution rate p_{min} and can be derived as follows from equation (4.50):

$$i_{eff} = \frac{f + p_{eff} + \rho^*}{1 - \rho^*} \tag{4.51}$$

$$i_{eff} \cdot (1 - \rho^*) = f + p_{eff} + \rho^* \tag{4.52}$$

$$p_{eff} = i_{eff} \cdot (1 - \rho^*) - f - \rho* \tag{4.53}$$

As is discernible from equation (4.53), p_{eff} may also assume negative values, and indeed if that happens, when i_{eff} is so small, that means:

$$p_{eff} < 0 \quad \text{if } i_{eff} < \frac{f + \rho^*}{1 - \rho^*} \tag{4.54}$$

Furthermore sensitivity analysis of p_{eff} versus i_{eff}

$$\frac{\partial p_{eff}}{\partial i_{eff}} = 1 - \rho^* \tag{4.55}$$

shows that, when the value of i_{eff} changes the value of p_{eff} does not change to the full extent of the value of i_{eff}, but only by the reduced factor of $1 - \rho^*$. That is because, in the case of a rise in the value of i_{eff}, this rise must also be covered again via a rise in the shortfall risk hedging rate, and vice versa. This will become clear in the following subsection.

4.6.3 Effective Shortfall Risk Hedging Rate

By analogy with the effective profit contribution rate, the effective shortfall risk hedging rate can be derived by using equation (4.14):

$$r_{eff} = \frac{\rho^*}{1 - \rho^*} \cdot (1 + f + p_{eff}) \tag{4.56}$$

Bringing equation (4.53) into use results in:

$$r_{eff} = \frac{\rho^*}{1 - \rho^*} \cdot (1 + f + i_{eff} \cdot (1 + \rho^*) - f - \rho^*) \tag{4.57}$$

$$r_{eff} = \frac{\rho^*}{1 - \rho^*} \cdot ((1 - \rho^*) + i_{eff} \cdot (1 - \rho^*)) \tag{4.58}$$

$$r_{eff} = \rho^* \cdot (1 + i_{eff}) \tag{4.59}$$

Because ρ^* and i_{eff} are always positive figures, it is always the case that:

$$r_{eff} > 0 \tag{4.60}$$

The sensitivity analysis of r_{eff} in relation to i_{eff},

$$\frac{\partial r_{eff}}{\partial i_{eff}} = \rho^* \tag{4.61}$$

shows that the value of r_{eff}, in the case of any change in the value of i_{eff} likewise does not change to the same extent as i_{eff}, but this time changes by the reduced factor ρ^*.

The sum of both partial differentials equations (4.55) and (4.61)

$$\frac{\partial p_{eff}}{\partial i_{eff}} + \frac{\partial r_{eff}}{\partial i_{eff}} = 1 - \rho^* + \rho^* = 1 \tag{4.62}$$

shows, as was to be expected, that any change in the value of i_{eff} is distributed completely over the values of p_{eff} and r_{eff}, and indeed in the ratio

$$\frac{\Delta p_{eff}}{\Delta r_{eff}} = \frac{1 - \rho^*}{\rho^*} \tag{4.63}$$

As ρ^* is substantially smaller than $(1 - \rho^*)$ in the case of borrowers of good financial standing, the essentially larger part of any change in the effective rate of interest on the effective profit contribution ratio does not apply.

4.6.4   Maximum Shortfall Risk Covered

In some Swiss cantons the maximum loan interest rate i_{max} for consumer credit is laid down by law. The question thus arises — up to what maximum credit shortfall risk ρ^* may consumer credit be granted in the case of a given minimum risk-free standard rate of interest I_{smin}? The following applies, using equation (4.49):

$$i_{max} = \frac{i_{smin} + \rho^*_{max}}{1 - \rho^*_{max}} \tag{4.64}$$

Solving, using ρ^*_{max}, results in:

$$\rho^*_{max} = \frac{i_{max} - i_{smin}}{1 + i_{max}} = \frac{i_{max} - f - p_{min}}{1 + i_{max}} \tag{4.65}$$

Equation (4.67) makes it clear that higher values for i_{max} permit higher values for ρ^*_{max} too. Moreover it is that case that:

$$\rho_{max} = 0 \quad \text{if } i_{max} = f + p_{min} \tag{4.66}$$

For the legislature laying down the value of i_{max}, the necessity arises from this that:

$$i_{max} \gg f + p_{min} \tag{4.67}$$

The market for consumer credit would otherwise be reduced to vanishing point owing to high credit-worthiness requirements.

4.7   RESULTS AND CONCLUSIONS

The shortfall risk hedging rate is normally calculated from the following equation according to Section 4.2:

$$r = \frac{\rho^*}{1 - \rho^*} \cdot (1 + i_{rf}) \tag{4.14}$$

In the case of current account lending a correction factor r_c must be introduced, depending on the average utilisation of the loan:

$$r_{cacj} = r_c \cdot \frac{\rho_j^*}{1 - \rho_j^*} \cdot (1 + r_{scac}) \tag{4.21}$$

We refer to the expositions in Section 4.5 for calculation of the correction factor.
The minimum loan interest rate is calculated from the equation:

$$i_{min} = \frac{i_{smin} + \rho^*}{1 - \rho^*} \tag{4.50}$$

This is one of the most significant equations. It is particularly important here to note the numerator. The greater the shortfall risk hedging rate, the more the numerator in equation (4.49) makes itself noticeable: the minimum loan interest rate is not simply the sum of the minimum risk-free standard rate of interest and of risk!

After the minimum rate of loan interest i_{min} has been laid down for a loan transaction, it will in practice be rounded up to the next normal round figure (usually in the form of one-quarter, one-eighth or one-sixteenth of 1%). This results in the effective loan interest rate i_{eff}. Thus the effective profit contribution rate and the effective shortfall risk hedging rate are calculated as follows:

$$p_{eff} = i_{eff} \cdot (1 - \rho^*) - f - \rho^* \tag{4.53}$$

$$r_{eff} = \rho^* \cdot (1 + i_{eff}) \tag{4.59}$$

There is an important observation here, that the effective profit contribution rate becomes negative under the condition:

$$i_{eff} < \frac{f + \rho^*}{1 - \rho^*} \tag{4.54}$$

The effective shortfall risk hedging rate may not, however, ever be negative!

4.8   EXAMPLE

It is intended to grant a borrower a fixed advance for one year. The starting position looks like this:

Financing cost rate: f $= 3.000\%$
Minimum profit contribution rate: $p_{min} = 1.000\%$
Credit shortfall risk: $\rho^* = 0.757\%$
(Rating BB according to Table 2.1)

The minimum risk-free standard rate of interest is:

$$i_{smin} = 3\% + 1\% = 4\%$$

The shortfall risk hedging rate, according to equation (4.14) is:

$$r = \frac{0.00757}{1 - 0.00757} \cdot (1 + 0.04) = 0.7933\%$$

From this is calculated the minimum loan interest rate according to equation (1.1) by

$$i_{min} = 4\% + 0.7933\% = 4.7933\%$$

One obtains the same result, moving directly, via the shortfall risk hedging rate r under equation (4.49):

$$i_{min} = \frac{0.04 + 0.00757}{1 - 0.00757} = 4.7933\%$$

The figure of 4.7933% is not customary in Swiss banking practice. It is therefore rounded up to the nearest eighth:

$$i_{eff} = 4\frac{7}{8}\% = 4.875\%$$

The effective profit contribution rate and the effective shortfall risk hedging rate are calculated, with the aid of equations (4.53) and (4.59), as follows:

$$p_{eff} = 0.04875 \cdot (1 - 0.00757) - 0.03 - 0.00757 = 1.0811\%$$
$$r_{eff} = 0.00757 \cdot (1 + 0.04875) = 0.7939\%$$

The proof is:

$$i_{eff} = 3\% + 1.0811\% + 0.7939\% = 4.875\% = 4\frac{7}{8}\%$$

5

Calculation of the Shortfall Risk Hedging Rate in the General Case of Variable Shortfall Risk

We now give up, in this chapter, the condition $\rho_1 = \cdots = \rho_n = \rho$. First the exact solution for the case of a fixed interest loan without repayments will be derived in Section 5.1. In Section 5.2 we will draw up, using an approximate solution as an example, a comparison with the special case in Chapter 4, and we will examine the accuracy of the approximate solution in Section 5.3.

Other important clean credits will be dealt with in Sections 5.4, 5.5 and 5.6. The important results and conclusions from Chapter 5 will be summarised in Section 5.7.

The aim of this chapter is to elaborate general principles, which will then be developed further in Chapter 7.

5.1 FIXED INTEREST LOAN WITHOUT REPAYMENTS

First it is intended to examine again, as in Chapter 4, the fixed advance without repayments. Equation (3.18) must, however, now be brought into play for the value ψ_j in equation (1.2). By analogy with equation (4.1) this results in (for cases where the loan is covered, the values are on the other hand valid when the collateral is included):

$$
\Lambda = \left(\sum_{j=1}^{n} \frac{i \cdot L \cdot \prod_{k=1}^{j}(1 - \rho_k)}{(1 + i_s)^j} \right) + \left(\frac{L \cdot \prod_{k=1}^{n}(1 - \rho_k)}{(1 + i_s)^n} \right)
$$

$$
+ \left(\sum_{j=1}^{n} \frac{b \cdot L \cdot (1 + i) \cdot \rho_j \cdot \prod_{k=1}^{j-1}(1 - \rho_k)}{(1 + i_s)^j} \right) \tag{5.1}
$$

The left-hand summand again corresponds to the discounted expectation values of the interest payments, the centre summand to the expectation value of the loan repayment and the right-hand summand to the sum of the discounted expectation values of the breakdown distributions. It will again be assumed, as in Chapter 4, that there is one uniform risk-free rate of interest i_s for all terms. $\Lambda = L$ will again be set (see Section 4.1) for the period in which the loan is paid out.

The following substitutions will be made in order to be make handling equation (5.1) more manageable:

$$x = \sum_{i=1}^{n} \frac{\prod_{k=1}^{j}(1 - \rho_k)}{(1 + i_s)^j} \tag{5.2}$$

$$y = \frac{\prod_{k=1}^{n}(1 - \rho_k)}{(1 + i_s)^n} \tag{5.3}$$

$$z = \sum_{j=1}^{n} \frac{\rho_j \cdot \prod_{k=1}^{j-1}(1 - \rho_u)}{(1 + i_s)^j} \tag{5.4}$$

With x, y and z brought into play, and abbreviated with L, there results:

$$1 = i \cdot x + y + b \cdot (1 + i) \cdot z \tag{5.5}$$

and solved using i:

$$i = \frac{1 - (y + b \cdot z)}{x + b \cdot z} \tag{5.6}$$

Logically, no further simplification of the representation can be achieved by any reverse substitution. Equations (5.2), (5.3), and (5.4) should therefore be seen as computational indications, the results of which may be brought into play in equation (5.6). These equations can be used with appropriate PC worksheets without any difficulty.

The mean shortfall risk ρ_m, which implicitly underlies the interest rate calculated in this way, is calculated as follows using equation (4.67) as an example:

$$\rho_m = \frac{i - i_s}{1 + i} \tag{5.7}$$

5.2   APPROXIMATE SOLUTION FOR FIXED INTEREST LOAN WITHOUT REPAYMENTS

The computing needs for Section 5.1 are in practice indeed applicable, but very unwieldy. An approximate solution is therefore derived in this section.

The shortfall risk ρ_k of the kth period can be replaced by the sum of the average shortfall risk ρ_a of all n periods and the kth deviation $\Delta\rho_k$ by this means:

$$\rho_k = \rho_a + \Delta\rho_k$$

$$\text{with } \rho_a = \frac{\sum_{k=1}^{n} \rho_k}{n} \tag{5.8}$$

Equations (5.2) for x, (5.3) for y and (5.4) for z now read:

$$x = \sum_{j=1}^{n} \frac{\prod_{k=1}^{j}(1 - [\rho_a + \Delta\rho_k])}{(1 + i_s)^j} \qquad (5.9)$$

$$y = \frac{\prod_{k=1}^{n}(1 - [\rho_a + \Delta\rho_k])}{(1 + i_s)^n} \qquad (5.10)$$

$$z = \sum_{j=1}^{n} \frac{(\rho_a + \Delta\rho_j) \cdot \prod_{k=1}^{j-1}(1 - [\rho_a + \Delta\rho_k])}{(1 + i_s)^j} \qquad (5.11)$$

The approximate solution is derived in Appendix 6 using conventional approximation equation. The result is:

$$i = \frac{i_s + \rho_a^*}{1 - \rho_a^*} \qquad (5.29)$$

Comparison with equation (4.49) shows that it is identical to equation (5.29). In the case of the variable ρ_j equation (4.49) may thus be used, likewise approximately, in that the constant ρ^* is replaced by the average ρ_a^*. On the basis of the type and method of derivation used, this result could indeed have been expected.

5.3   RELIABILITY OF THE APPROXIMATE SOLUTION

At this point the reliability of the approximate solution will be illustrated by means of six numerical examples. Let's put $i_s = 5\%$, $\rho_a^* = 1\%$ and $b = 0$ in all the examples. The approximate solution is thus always $i = 6.0606\%$. The values for the shortfall risk ρ concerned in the individual years may be taken from Table 5.1. The value of i, calculated precisely, is detailed in the third column from the right-hand side and may be compared with the approximate solution $i = 6.0606\%$.

The examples were selected as follows:

- a and d represent deteriorating credit-worthiness
- b and e represent improving credit-worthiness

Table 5.1   Reliability of the approximate solution

	Values for ρ_k year					Results		
	1	2	3	4	5	$i_{\text{exact}}(\%)$	abs. error	rel. error
a	0.8%	0.9%	1.0%	1.1%	1.2%	6.0481%	0.0125%	0.2062%
b	1.2%	1.1%	1.0%	0.9%	0.8%	6.0733%	−0.0127%	−0.2092%
c	1.0%	1.1%	1.0%	0.9%	1.0%	6.0631%	−0.0025%	−0.0418%
d	0.6%	0.8%	1.0%	1.2%	1.4%	6.0359%	0.0247%	0.4093%
e	1.4%	1.2%	1.0%	0.8%	0.6%	6.0863%	−0.0257%	−0.4215%
f	1.0%	0.8%	1.0%	1.2%	1.0%	6.0557%	0.0049%	0.0816%

- c and f represent oscillating credit-worthiness
- in c there is deterioration at first and in f there is improvement at first
- in a, b and c the changes in each case are half the size of those in d, e and f.

The following can be seen from the results:

- The approximate value for i is too high in the case of deteriorating credit-worthiness, and too low in the case of improving credit-worthiness.
- In the case of oscillating credit-worthiness it depends whether it has improved at first (approximate solution too high) or deteriorated first (approximate solution too low).
- The deviation of the approximate solution is about double in the case of changes that are double the size.
- Although great fluctuations in credit-worthiness were inserted into the examples, the absolute error amounts to only a few basis points or fractions of a basis point.

As has already been emphasised in Section 5.1, it is possible to use the exact equations with appropriate PC worksheets. In most cases, however, usable results can also be delivered by approximate solution.

5.4   FIXED ADVANCE WITH COMPLETE REPAYMENT

Equation (1.2) appears in this case as follows:

$$\Lambda = \sum_{j=1}^{n}$$

$$\times \frac{\left\{i \cdot L \cdot \left[1 - \frac{(j-1)}{n}\right] + \frac{L}{n}\right\} \cdot \prod_{k=1}^{j}(1 - \rho_k) + b \cdot \rho_j \cdot \left\{(1+i) \cdot L \cdot \left[1 - \frac{(j-1)}{n}\right]\right\} \cdot \prod_{k=1}^{j-1}(1 - \rho_k)}{(1 + i_s)^j}$$

(5.30)

The first summand in the numerator corresponds to the expectation values of the interest payments and repayments. The first summand in the left-hand curved brackets corresponds to the interest payments, with the square brackets detailing the rest of the loan subject to interest in each case. The second summand in the left-hand curved brackets corresponds to the tranche of repayment. The second summand in the numerator corresponds to the expectation values of the breakdown distributions. The square brackets in the right-hand curved brackets represents the remaining debt. The other terms are analogous to those in equation (5.1).

The result for i is derived in Appendix 6 on the assumption that $\Lambda = L$ at the time of paying out. The result is:

$$i = \frac{n}{\sum_{j=1}^{n} \frac{\left[\left(1 + \left(\frac{b \cdot \rho_j}{1 - \rho_j}\right) \cdot \left(1 + \frac{1}{i}\right)\right) \cdot (n - j + 1) + \frac{1}{i}\right] \cdot \prod_{k=1}^{j}(1 - \rho_k)}{(1 + i_s)^j}}$$

(5.38)

Table 5.2 Interest rate comparison for loans with and without repayments

Example	$i_{\text{without amo}}$	$i_{\text{with amo}}$	i_{with} less i_{without}
a	6.0481%	5.9798%	−0.0683%
b	6.0733%	6.1418%	0.0685%
c	6.0631%	6.0768%	0.0137%
d	6.0359%	5.8994%	−0.1365%
e	6.0863%	6.2234%	0.1371%
f	6.0557%	6.0284%	−0.0273%

The rate of interest i in equation (5.38) occurs both to the left and to the right of the equals sign. In this format the equation is therefore soluble iteratively with the aid of an appropriate PC worksheet.

In order to illustrate equation (5.38), the interest rates for fixed advances with repayments in Table 5.2 are calculated with the risks over term examples of Table 5.1 and compared with the rate of interest of fixed advances without repayments. The standard rate of interest i_s is again 5%.

It is now interesting to realise that lower interest rates result only in examples a, d and f in the case of repayments. These are the cases of deteriorating credit-worthiness. Here repayments clearly have the effect of reducing risk. In the cases of improving credit-worthiness it is the other way round. In these cases, because lower amounts of loan are bearing interest on account of repayments in periods of good credit-worthiness, only correspondingly lower revenues may be billed. The result of this is that a higher margin is needed at the beginning of the term of the loan, which leads to higher rates of interest in relation to loans without repayments.

5.5 FIXED ADVANCE WITH PARTIAL REPAYMENTS

Equation (5.23) has to be supplemented as follows for this case:

$$
L = \sum_{j=1}^{n}
$$

$$
\times \frac{\left\{ i \cdot L \cdot \left[1 - \frac{\alpha \cdot (j-1)}{n} \right] + \frac{\alpha \cdot L}{n} \right\} \cdot \prod_{k=1}^{j}(1 - \rho_k) + b \cdot \rho_j \cdot \left\{ (1+i) \cdot L \cdot \left[1 - \frac{\alpha \cdot (j-1)}{n} \right] \right\} \cdot \prod_{k=1}^{j-1}(1 - \rho_k)}{(1 + i_s)^j}
$$

$$
+ \frac{(1 - \alpha) \cdot L \cdot \prod_{k=1}^{n}(1 - \rho_k)}{(1 + i_s)^n} \tag{5.39}
$$

Here α represents the degree of repayment with $0 < \alpha \leq 1$. The solution path matches that in the preceding section and leads once more to an iterative solution. We will not go into the derivation at this point. The solution lies in each case between that for loans without repayments and that for loans with complete repayments over the term.

5.6   CURRENT ACCOUNT LOANS

As interest rates on current account loans may be adjusted in the short term to new circumstances, there is no problem regarding changes in the borrower's credit-worthiness. As soon as the bank establishes such situations, it simply recalculates and adjusts the loan interest rate.

5.7   RESULTS AND CONCLUSIONS

As Tables 5.1 and 5.2 show, real-life loans may normally be handled by using the average shortfall risk ρ_a according to equation (5.8), in conjunction with the equations given in Chapter 4. If it is suspected that this approximation is insufficiently accurate, this chapter supplies the details needed to check the approximation or to calculate interest rates more precisely.

The results to date are only applicable as an autonomous model if the bank has the necessary statistical data available. It also needs an operational accounting system, such as is normally found in insurance companies, in order to be able to calculate the parameters used in the model in relation to the past. Forecasts for the future can be drawn up supported by these and the corresponding values inserted into the model. Chapter 6 outlines how to go about this.

Above all, however, the calculations we have made so far serve as a basis on which to develop further the approach of Black and Scholes [BLSC73, S. 673 and thereafter] in Chapter 7. Equations (4.49) and (5.29) form the necessary prerequisites for this.

6

Shortfall Risk on Uncovered Loans on the Basis of Statistics

This chapter will open up opportunities for determining the shortfall risks of borrowers with the aid of statistics. Experience in Swiss bank lending shows that loans to businesses and to private individuals more or less balance out, both in terms of numbers and in terms of amounts. Separate and detailed consideration of both these groups of customers is therefore justified.

6.1 PRIVATE CLIENTS

As will be shown in Chapter 8, the shortfall risk of covered loans — as these predominantly are in the case of private client business (mortgages, loans against other collateral) — is made up of the shortfall risk for uncovered loans to the same borrowers and of the shortfall risk of the cover. The shortfall risk for loans to private clients on an uncovered basis will therefore be examined below. (Domowitz and Sartain have as it happens established in a recent study for the USA [DOSA97], that invoices for medical services and credit card balances represent the most frequent cause of personal bankruptcy. A development that may possibly be in store for Switzerland too?)

Private individuals normally have four possible sources of income with which to finance their debt servicing:

- income from salaried employment
- income from self employment
- pensions (old age and dependant's insurance, pension funds, life insurance, etc.)
- investment income and assets

Earned income and pensions are normally mutually exclusive and may thus be considered separately. Investment income comes, when there is any, on top of them. Any loan to a private individual is subject to default if the person concerned no longer has sufficient income available to service the debt. The various sources of income and the effects they have on the shortfall risk will be examined separately below.

6.1.1 Unearned Income and Income from Self-employment

The shortfall risk of the private individual in these cases corresponds to the shortfall risk of the pension fund or of his/her own company. It will therefore be referred to in Section 6.2 instead.

6.1.2   Income from Salaried Employment

It is assumed in this subsection that the bank will grant a private individual an uncovered loan amounting to L_s on the strength of his/her salary. The size of the loan L_s in relation to salary is determined on the basis of the bank's credit policy. A defensive attitude by the bank may, in an extreme case, take the form of uncovered loans not being granted to private individuals in principle. That would, however, also mean not granting any normal consumer credit either! Establishment of loan amount L_s therefore takes place in line with appropriate practice, taking account of salary in accordance with the normal rules of consumer credit business. The size of L_s is thus aligned with the acceptability of the debt servicing potential.

The bank's risk here is that the borrower becomes unemployed and remains so in the long term. Short-term unemployment can usually be bridged with the aid of unemployment insurance. The probability of the borrower becoming unemployed in the long term within one year can be investigated on the basis of unemployment figures relating to his/her occupation, age and location. From this the bank must then determine for itself whether this probability is more or less likely to befall the borrower concerned over the next year. Economic forecasts for the occupational or professional group concerned and for the region, as well as the personal qualifications of the borrower, play a decisive role in this. This is obviously not easy, but the bank nonetheless has to form a view for itself.

In addition to the risk of unemployment, the risks of invalidity and death have to be taken into account. Appropriate policies may, however, be taken out with the insurance industry to cover these risks, and these may be assigned in favour of the loan. We will not therefore go further into these risks at this point.

6.1.3   Investment Income and Assets

This subsection will distinguish on the one hand between securities and credit balance assets, and property assets on the other hand.

Revenues from securities and credit balance assets are often very volatile. The probability of a person defaulting on an uncovered loan that is backed up solely by income from assets must therefore be considered very high. If a private borrower only has income from securities and credit balances available, then the shortfall risk should be calculated only on the basis of covering the loan. Loans that a bank may make against other collateral should be evaluated according to appropriate statistics.

The case of income arising from returns on real property is quite different. Long-term and sustained revenue can be perfectly well achieved from real property, and can be very precisely estimated on the basis of experience in the property sector. The risk for the bank consists in the possibility of the management of the property in question being improperly conducted, and of its long-term revenue thus being jeopardised. Such cases have a feature in common and comparable with that of companies. In the case of returns from property in private ownership, a 'management agreement' can be drawn up, as indeed has already been done on occasion. This then becomes a situation for review, as will be described in Section 6.2.

6.2 COMPANIES

Historically orientated definitions of the probability of a company defaulting on a loan can be made on the basis of bankruptcy statistics. In order to arrive at the most precise figures possible for individual companies it is necessary to classify the entirety of all companies as neatly as possible. Here it makes sense to weigh up against each other the need for the neatest possible classification and the need for results that are statistically meaningful. Particular criteria for classification are:

- business sectors
- geographical/economic areas
- sizes of enterprises by number(s) of employees
- how long companies have been established

Such details may be obtained — for foreign companies too — and are included in every census of business operations in Switzerland. The most intractable problem is certainly classification by sectors, as many companies clearly cannot simply be fitted into just one particular sector.

How far back the necessary period for consideration should go depends on the size of the individual segments, and on the need to obtain statistically meaningful results. On the other hand the observation period should not be too long, in order to have facts that are as up to date as possible, and which provide clues that will be applicable for the following period.

Analysing bankruptcy statistics always involves reappraisal of the past but, on the other hand, the future is far from simply being an extrapolation of it.

Banks cannot therefore avoid forming an opinion on the risks of defaults arising in individual segments over the coming periods concerned, based on the one hand on historical (but reappraised) facts and on the other hand on economic forecasts.

The facts behind the bankruptcy statistics should be as up to date as possible for the purposes described above. The degree of relevance required is not necessarily provided by facts that are made available from official sources. On the strength of their high market shares the major banks, in particular, and the cantonal banks within their cantonal areas, should, however, have sufficiently accurate facts at their disposal, even if they only use them for making evaluations within their own established clientele.

We will not go any further into such statistical methods here. We refer you at this point to appropriate specialist reading (such as [BOHL92]).

Part III
Option-Theory Loan Risk Model

Shortfall risk on uncovered loans to companies on the basis of an option-theory approach

Loans covered against shortfall risk

Calculation of the combination of loans with the lowest interest costs

7

Shortfall Risk on Uncovered Loans to Companies on the Basis of an Option-Theory Approach

There are some hurdles to be cleared, as has been shown in Section 6.2, when it comes to the statistical determination of the shortfall risk of uncovered loans to companies. The relevance and necessary scope of the facts is uncertain. The individual assessment of any one company is only possible by cross-comparison, in so far as the facts needed may exist. The largely inadmissible extrapolation from the past into the future can only be avoided by using economic forecasts, for which the appropriate facts and contexts have to be known.

This cannot be satisfactory. We therefore introduce a fundamentally different way forward in this chapter. A company will be individually assessed, using an option-theory approach, on the basis of operational information. As a second step it will be demonstrated, on the strength of analogous conclusions, how loans to private individuals may be assessed too.

7.1 DIFFERENCE IN APPROACH BETWEEN BLACK/SCHOLES AND KMV, TOGETHER WITH FURTHER ELABORATION

It was Black and Scholes who first described the equity of a company partly financed by outside capital as a call-option and the debts as risk-free credit, combined with a put-option on the total value of the company [BLSC73, S. 637 and thereafter]. In this their reflections were based on the assumption that the outside capital was made available in the form of a zero bond. Cox and Rubinstein [CORU85, S. 375 and thereafter] described this approached later, with further refinements. More recently this approach has been taken up again by Grenadier [GREN96].

As already mentioned in Section 1.2, the KMV Corporation in San Francisco, California, USA, is adopting a similar approach (see [VAS184] and [KAEL98]. Here an inference was made from the volatility of the stockmarket prices of listed companies to the volatility of their values. Their model does not, however, use the Black/Scholes formula, but pursues, starting likewise from a stochastic process, a similar solution approach. In contrast to this, the volatility of the capitalised free cash flows will be used, in the context of this study, to assess the volatility of values of the company, and the Black/Scholes formula will be used as a model. Loans to non-listed companies may thereby be assessed also.

The Black/Scholes approach is developed further here, with debts no longer being examined in the form of a zero bond. It will rather be assumed here that the repayment of the loan paid out L plus the agreed interest at the rate of i is owed at the end of any period of time. This is completely permissible, as the nominal value of a zero bond may also be seen as its market value with interest on it accrued. Every investor is taking, as the basis for an investment in zero bonds, a yield to be achieved that determined the relationship between market value and nominal value. This consideration leads logically to the conclusion that the nominal value of the zero bond may be replaced by the magnitude $\Lambda \cdot (1 + i)$, in which Λ corresponds to the current market value and i. corresponds to the return on the market value set by the investor over the remainder of the term. In applying these considerations to loans, $\Lambda = L$ will be put in again, as we did in Sections 4.1 and 5.1. The nominal value X of the zero bonds according to the notation by Black/Scholes may thus be seen as shorthand for $X = L \cdot (1 + i)$. The result has to be the same in the end. A generalised solution is, however, obtained by applying equations (4.49) and (5.29) respectively.

As will be demonstrated in this chapter, this approach leads to a solution for the risk-adjusted loan interest rate which, in contrast to that of Black/Scholes, is independent of the risk-free rate of interest i_s. It becomes possible, therefore — unlike the approach of Black/Scholes — to assess debt structures that may be as complicated as you like, in a simple way. In Chapter 8 we will see that it is also possible to assess companies that have taken up both covered and uncovered loans at the same time.

The fundamental of the methods being developed here will be explained first, in the next section. The derivation and discussion of the risk-adjusted loan interest rate at the time of establishing the loan conditions will follow in Sections 7.3 to 7.6. The intermediate assessment of outstanding credit will be discussed in Sections 7.7 and 7.8, and the influence of the privileged wages and salaries payable in the event of bankruptcy, under Switzerland's laws concerning the pursuit of debt and bankruptcy, will be examined in Section 7.9. Section 7.10 will specify the limits on the application of the method presented here, and the most important results will be portrayed in Section 7.11. The final section, 7.12, application of the method will be illustrated with the aid of examples.

7.2 DERIVATION OF BASIC FORMULAE

First of all debts are assumed to be in the form of one single bank loan, in which at the end of a period the nominal value L plus the agreed interest at the rate of i will become due for payment according to the period concerned. The length of the period of time will first of all be consciously left open. This is permissible, if the rate of interest i corresponds to the length of the period. On the basis of these assumptions the following possible values result at the end of the period for the equity and for the debt, following on [CORU85, S. 377]:

$$E = \text{Max}(V - L \cdot (1 + i); 0) \tag{7.1}$$

$$D = \text{Min}(V; L \cdot (1 + i)) \tag{7.2}$$

$$V = E + D \tag{7.3}$$

$E =$ equity
$D =$ debts
$V =$ value of the company

At the end of the period the market value of the company's equity corresponds either to the company's market value V less the bank's demand $L \cdot (1 + i)$ — or it is, in the case of the

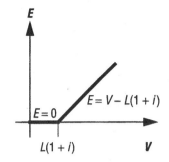

Figure 7.1

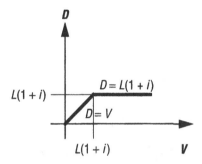

Figure 7.2

bank's demand being higher than the company's market value, equal to zero. This is expressed in equation (7.1).

On the other hand, at the end of the term of the loan the bank receives either its demand $L \cdot (1 + i)$ paid back, or the owners of the company let it go bankrupt, as it is not worthwhile for them to pay back a loan demand that is higher than the company's market value. In this situation it is more advantageous for the owners of the company to invest the money in a new enterprise.

Debts and the market value of equity together result in the company's value according to equation (7.3). Figures 7.1 and 7.2 show the situation at the end of the loan's term.

From Figure 7.1 it becomes evident that the market value of equity is no different from the equivalent of a European call option on the company's market value. On the other hand, according to Figures 7.2, 7.3 and 7.4, the debts may also be portrayed as a risk-free investment with the value $L \cdot (1 + i)$ plus a European put option written on the company's market value. The unexpired term of these options corresponds in each case to the time until the loan falls due [CORU85, S. 380].

On the basis of the figures it becomes furthermore clear that $L \cdot (1 + i)$ corresponds to the striking price and V to the basic value of the option. The call put parity leads to, with P corresponding with the value of the put:

$$E = P + V - L \cdot (1 + i) \cdot (1 + i_s)^{-1} \tag{7.4}$$

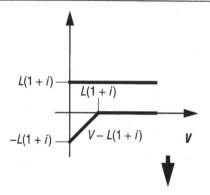

Figure 7.3

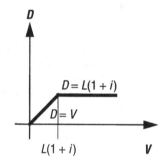

Figure 7.4

The value for the risk-free standard rate of interest i_s must of course be put in, likewise matching the period of time. It works out for the company's value V as follows:

$$V = L \cdot \left(\frac{1+i}{1+i_s} \right) + E - P \tag{7.5}$$

The value of the debts works out, using equation (7.3), as follows:

$$D = V - E = L \cdot \left(\frac{1+i}{1+i_s} \right) - P \tag{7.6}$$

The expression $L \cdot (1+i) \cdot (1+i_s)^{-1}$ is no different from the fully discounted nominal value of the loan plus interest. This value may now be compared with the value of the debts. The quotient of the expectation value and of the fully discounted nominal value of the loan demand is here no different from the survival chance of the loan taking into account breakdown distributions.

$$\chi^* = \frac{D}{L \cdot \left(\frac{1+i}{1+i_s} \right)} = 1 - \rho^* \tag{7.7}$$

Equation (7.6) substituted into equation (7.7) results in:

$$1 - \rho^* = \frac{L \cdot \left(\frac{1+i}{1+i_s}\right) - P}{L \cdot \left(\frac{1+i}{1+i_s}\right)} \qquad (7.8)$$

Further transformations lead to:

$$(1 - \rho^*) \cdot L \cdot \left(\frac{1+i}{1+i_s}\right) = L \cdot \left(\frac{1+i}{1+i_s}\right) - P \qquad (7.9)$$

$$L \cdot \left(\frac{1+i}{1+i_s}\right) - \rho^* \cdot L \cdot \left(\frac{1+i}{1+i_s}\right) = L \cdot \left(\frac{1+i}{1+i_s}\right) - P \qquad (7.10)$$

$$\rho^* \cdot L \cdot \left(\frac{1+i}{1+i_s}\right) = P \qquad (7.11)$$

$$\rho^* = \frac{P}{L \cdot \left(\frac{1+i}{1+i_s}\right)} \qquad (7.12)$$

Equations (7.11) and (7.12) give in detail the correlation between the put value and the credit shortfall risk probability taking breakdown distributions into account.

7.3 DERIVATION OF RISK-ADJUSTED VALUES

First the assumption is made of a company that has its debts position only in the form of a bank loan. If it is intended that the loan interest rate i be risk adjusted, then the value of the debts corresponds, in the case of only one bank loan, to its nominal value:

$$D = L \qquad (7.13)$$

By substituting equation (7.6) into equation (7.13) one obtains:

$$L = L \cdot \left(\frac{1+i}{1+i_s}\right) - P \qquad (7.14)$$

Now comes the decisive difference from the approaches to date made by Black/Scholes and Merton. With the aid of equation (4.49), which demonstrates the relation between the risk-free standard rate of interest i_s, the shortfall risk ρ^* and the risk-adjusted rate of interest i, the quotient in the brackets of equation (7.14) may be remodelled.

$$\frac{1+i}{1+i_s} = \frac{1 + \frac{i_s + \rho^*}{1 - \rho^*}}{1 + i_s} = \frac{1 - \rho^* + i_s + \rho^*}{(1 + i_s) \cdot (1 - \rho^*)} = \frac{1 + i_s}{(1 + i_s) \cdot (1 - \rho^*)} \qquad (7.15)$$

The result reads:

$$\frac{1+i}{1+i_s} = \frac{1}{1 - \rho^*} \qquad (7.16)$$

Substituted into equation (7.14) this gives:

$$L = \frac{L}{(1 - \rho^*)} - P \tag{7.17}$$

Elimination from equation (7.17) using ρ^* leads to:

$$\rho^* = \frac{P}{L + P} \tag{7.18}$$

From this it follows that the credit shortfall risk for the calculation of the risk-adjusted loan interest rate is known, if one succeeds in calculating the value of the put.

According to equation (7.18) it follows from $P = 0$ that $\rho^* = 0$, and for $P = \infty$ that $\rho^* = 1$. All values that P may assume thus result in a permissible value for ρ^*, and vice versa.

To test this, the credit shortfall risk starting from equation (7.12) will be calculated once more. Equation (7.12) is, with the help of equation (7.16) expressed as follows:

$$\rho^* = \frac{P}{L \cdot \left(\frac{1}{1 - \rho^*}\right)} \tag{7.19}$$

Extended by $(1 - \rho^*)$ results in:

$$\rho^* = \frac{P \cdot (1 - \rho^*)}{L} \tag{7.20}$$

Further transformations result in:

$$\rho^* \cdot L = P - \rho^* \cdot P \tag{7.21}$$

$$\rho^* \cdot (L + P) = P \tag{7.22}$$

$$\rho^* = \frac{P}{L + P} \tag{7.23}$$

The comparison shows that equations (7.18) and (7.23) are identical.

What is essentially new in the approach presented here is that the relation between i_s, i and ρ^* according to equation (7.16) is used, first to calculate the credit shortfall risk ρ^*, detached from the risk-free standard rate of interest i_s and from the loan interest rate i. This is the small detour, already mentioned in Chapter 1, which does, however, lead in what follows to the general solution.

If $\chi^* = 1 - \rho^*$ (see equation (2.8)) is calculated first, the later calculations can be simplified. Under equations (7.18) and (7.23) it is the case that:

$$1 - \chi^* = \frac{P}{L + P} \tag{7.24}$$

Transformations result in:

$$L + P - \chi^*(L + P) = P \tag{7.25}$$

$$\chi^* \cdot (L + P) = L \tag{7.26}$$

$$\chi^* = \frac{L}{L + P} \tag{7.27}$$

According to Black/Scholes, for a period of time following on [CORU85, S. 211], the value of P amounts to:

$$P = L \cdot \frac{(1+i)}{(1+i_s)} \cdot N(x) - V \cdot N(x - \sigma) \qquad (7.28)$$

$$\text{with: } x = \frac{\ln\left(\frac{L \cdot (1+i)}{V \cdot (1+i_s)}\right)}{\sigma} + \frac{\sigma}{2} \qquad (7.29)$$

$N =$ standard normal distribution function
$\sigma =$ volatility of the company value according to the time period

On this we make the assumption here that the alternative investment might be made at the i_s rate of interest. This is the equivalent of granting credit to a borrower that would be, for the bank, risk-free. As such borrowers do not in reality exist this assumption might appear fanciful. This is not, however, the case, as the following consideration indicates: the alternative investment is made again at the risk-adjusted rate of interest to a borrower that is real and does exist. If the rate of interest is in fact established as risk adjusted, the bank's yield on this investment is, after deduction of losses, again equivalent to the rate of interest i_s. This means, in other words, that a bank's yield in any loan transaction always corresponds to the risk-free standard rate of interest i_s, providing the loan interest rate i is in fact calculated so that it is risk adjusted. The i_s may thus take over the function of the risk-free rate of interest in terms of being a model in the context of the lending operations of any bank.

With the definition of debt rate

$$d = \frac{L}{V} \qquad (7.30)$$

$d =$ debt rate

equation (7.27) expresses itself, by applying equations (7.28), (7.16) and (2.8) abbreviated to V, as follows:

$$\chi^* = \frac{d}{d + \frac{d}{\chi^*} \cdot N(x) - N(x - \sigma)} \qquad (7.31)$$

Multiplying out results in:

$$\chi^* \cdot (d - N(x - \sigma)) + d \cdot N(x) = d \qquad (7.32)$$

Reverse substitution $\chi^* = 1 - \rho^*$ results in:

$$(1 - \rho^*) \cdot (d - N(x - \sigma)) = d \cdot (1 - N(x)) \qquad (7.33)$$
$$\rho^* \cdot (d - N(x - \sigma)) = d - N(x - \sigma) - d + d \cdot N(x) \qquad (7.34)$$
$$\rho^* = \frac{d \cdot N(x) - N(x - \sigma)}{d - N(x - \sigma)} \qquad (7.35)$$
$$\text{with: } x = \frac{\ln\left(\frac{d}{1 - \rho^*}\right)}{\sigma} + \frac{\sigma}{2} \qquad (7.36)$$

As ρ^* also occurs in the expression for x, the set of equations (7.35)–(7.36) must be solved iteratively. This presents no problem with today's standard PC software (for example Microsoft Excel Release 4 or higher, see Appendix 2).

The approximation [CORU85, S. 205] $N(x) \approx N \cdot (x - s) \approx 1$ applies where $d/(1 - \rho^*) \gg 1$. It follows from this that $\rho^* = 1$. This means that ρ^* approaches 1 for high degrees of outside indebtedness.

In the reverse case, where $d/(1 - \rho^*) \ll 1$, the approximation $N(x) \approx N \cdot (x - s) \approx 0$ applies. It follows from this that $\rho^* \approx 0$. This means if the outside indebtedness approaches zero, the credit shortfall risk is also approaching zero.

Highly interesting is the fact that the credit shortfall risk ρ^* is now only dependent on the degree of outside indebtedness d and on the volatility σ of the company's market value. As the volatility is, however, dependent on the time period and/or loan term under consideration, the duration of these also has matching influence. In particular the credit shortfall risk is, however, not dependent on the risk-free standard rate of interest i_s! This is the essential difference from the Black/Scholes result using the zero bond approach [CORU85, S. 382].

The term of the loan that has been newly paid out, and/or the remaining term of a loan that it is intended to reassess, may be chosen as the period of time. Volatility relating to one year will be assumed for σ, as it is annual accounts and budgets that are normally evaluated in the context of loan assessment. The solution thus runs as follows:

$$\rho^*(t) = \frac{N(x - \sigma \cdot \sqrt{t}) - d \cdot N(x)}{N(x - \sigma \cdot \sqrt{t}) - d} \tag{7.37}$$

$$\text{with: } x = \frac{\ln\left(\frac{d}{1 - \rho^*(t)}\right)}{\sigma \cdot \sqrt{t}} + \frac{\sigma \cdot \sqrt{t}}{2} \tag{7.38}$$

t = loan/term

It is important to note here that $\rho^*(t)$ is calculated with equations (7.37–7.38). $\rho^*(t)$ is thus the probability of credit shortfall over the whole loan term. This value has to be converted to the mean credit shortfall risk per annum, aided by the rules for transforming notice periods (Section 3.2), in order to be able to calculate the annual rate of interest.

$$\rho^*_{pa} = 1 - \sqrt[t]{1 - \rho^*(t)} \tag{7.39}$$

The annual rate of interest consistent with risk can then be calculated with the aid of equation (4.49):

$$i_{pa} \frac{i_{spa} + \rho^*_{pa}}{1 - \rho^*_{pa}} \tag{7.40}$$

i_{pa} = interest rate on annual basis
i_{spa} = risk-free interest rate on annual basis
ρ^*_{pa} = average annual credit shortfall risk

The annual volatility should be inserted here for σ, and the term in years for t. If various new loans with different terms are granted to a company, then the appropriate credit shortfall risk must be decided for each term and proceeded with as described above.

In the case of current account loans, the time between two assessment dates should be inserted for t, i.e. normally one year. It follows from this, however, that the submission of intermediate accounts has an improving effect on credit-worthiness, as the bank's time for reaction becomes shorter, and a correspondingly shorter period may be inserted into the formula for t. It lines up with the current banking practice of demanding intermediate accounts of borrowers at higher risk. As has been shown, this makes complete sense.

It is still being assumed, on the basis of the approach used here, that loan interest is only paid for the whole term of the loan when the loan is repayable. This is of course not always the case! What does this now imply for the application of the method described here? Even if interest payments become payable during the term of a loan, it may happen that the borrower is not in a position to pay them. Owing to his inability to make interest payments, the borrower may thus already go bankrupt, before the loan itself is in default. This is not taken into account here. That, by implication, means the following:

- Either, that the probability that the borrower already goes bankrupt owing to a loan interest payment becoming due, is so small that it may be ignored,
- Or, that the borrower has been given time to make the interest payments, possibly until the repayment of the loan is due.

Only empirical investigations may show whether or not these implicit assumptions are permissible. At this point the supposition may merely be expressed that they do apply; it may in all probability be assumed that this first assumption applies in the case of firms of good financial standing. The second assumption will, however, always apply in the case of firms of poor financial standing, if the bank extending the credit is justified in hoping for a recovery in the situation. If there is no such hope, then it makes no difference if the borrower goes bankrupt earlier or only when repayment of the loan becomes due. If the put remains in the money in any case, it does not have to be waited for. Compare this to Brealey and Meyers [BRMY96, S. 668].

In Section 11.3 we demonstrate, with the help of a real-life example, how interest payments and loan repayments may be taken into account prior to expiry of the loan term.

7.4 DETERMINATION OF THE VALUES FOR THE SOLUTION FORMULA

This chapter is concerned with giving the user of our method useful hints on how it may be applied in practice. For this it is assumed that the borrower's track record and budget documentation are available to the user. First we explain how to proceed when the borrower is a company. The analogous conclusion of how to proceed for a private borrower is put forward in a final subsection.

7.4.1 The Value of the Company and its Debt Rate

The expositions in this subsection are based on explanations by Brealey and Meyers [BRMY96]. The debt-free company serves as a starting point for our considerations. In this case the market value of the assets corresponds to the market value of the equity, as the owners of the equity do not have to fulfil any expectations for providers of outside capital.

According to Brealey and Meyers, the value of a company may be determined by discounting its free cash flows and totalling the resulting values [BRMY96, S. 71/71]. The free cash flow is here defined as revenue less costs less investments [BRMY96, S. 71]:

Free cash flow = Revenues − Costs before interest and taxation − Investments

It is important to emphasise at this point that the free cash flow is calculated with costs included *prior to interest and taxation*. We are indeed concerned here at first to determine the value of the assets alone, without bring the liabilities side of the company's balance sheet into the picture at all!

In the notation being used in this study, the value of companies is therefore calculated as follows [BRMY96, S. 72]:

$$V = \sum_{n=1}^{\infty} \frac{C}{(1 + i_d)^n} \qquad (7.41)$$

C = free cash flow
i_d = discount rate

The total according to equation (7.41) is calculated as follows [BRMY96, S. 49]:

$$V = \frac{C}{i_d} \qquad (7.42)$$

(but also compare equation (7.46) and the statements made there).

The discount rate used according to equation (7.42) is, along with free cash flow, of decisive importance. It would, however, go far beyond the scope of this study to go any more closely into the determination of the discount rate at this juncture. Suffice is to point out here that in today's literature, despite some shortcomings that are widely recognised, the CAPM (capital asset pricing model) is as favoured as ever:

$$i_d = i_g + \beta(i_{mt} - i_g) \qquad (7.43)$$

β = measurement of unleveraged assets market risk according to CAPM
i_g = return on a risk-free investment in government bonds
i_{mt} = return on the market

We refer you to the literature concerned for further expositions on the CAPM, for example [BRMY96, S. 143–236].

The debt rate, which comes into place for the method described here, is therefore calculated as follows:

$$d = \frac{L}{V} = \frac{i_d \cdot L}{C} \qquad (7.44)$$

Summarising, let it be emphasised that it is a question, in the case of C, of the average, future free cash flow of the company.

An importance consequence ensues from equation (7.44): the debt rate relevant to lending is independent of the debt rate used for accounting. Only the discounted future free cash flows count. This may mean, in an extreme case, that a company that is today overloaded with debt according to its books may still be credit-worthy, provided its future prospects are otherwise good. The method being described does therefore provide the answer in relation to the extent to which it may be worth restructuring a company that is, according to its books, overloaded with debt.

Recently Cho [CHO98] has shown, with the aid of empirical investigations, that the structure of the company's ownership does, when all is said and done, have influence on the company's value.

This study shows once more how complex is the question of valuing companies. Whether the very simple procedure we sketch out is sufficient to do justice to the method described here, only empirical enquiries will show.

7.4.2 Volatility

In order to gain some idea of the volatility of a company it may, on the one hand, be ascertained on the basis of historical data. Here again, however, it is the case that the future is no simple extrapolation of the past. Better to combine the two, using annual accounts going back three or four years and one to two future-orientated budgets, even though these are associated with uncertainties. On a purely theoretical basis alone, however, it is not possible to lay down how volatility should be determined correctly for the purposes of the model. This can only be determined with the help of empirical investigations (see Chapter 10).

Substantially better results in determining volatility could be achieved if borrowers produced accounts every six months or even quarterly. But this is often not the case, as considerable work would be involved and no one apart from banks would be asking for them. As long as there are banks that do not insist on intermediate accounts this is not going to gain acceptance in the market. If such intermediate accounts did exist, substantially longer series of facts would be available for recently observed periods of time and results would improve accordingly. In so far as intermediate accounts do exist, it is therefore recommended that they be used.

The concrete calculation of annual volatility takes place by analogy with the method that was described by Cox and Rubinstein [CORU85, S. 254 and thereafter]:

$$\sigma = \frac{\Gamma\left(\frac{n-1}{2}\right)}{\Gamma\left(\frac{n}{2}\right)} \cdot \sqrt{\frac{1}{2} \cdot \sum_{k=1}^{n}\left(\ln\left(\frac{V_{k+1}}{V_k}\right) - \mu\right)^2} \tag{7.45}$$

$$\mu = \frac{1}{n} \cdot \sum_{k=1}^{n} \ln\left(\frac{V_{k+1}}{V_k}\right)$$

n = number of quotients of annual reports and budgets
Γ = gamma function
μ = medium of the logarithms

The gamma function values are of interest as shown in Table 7.1 [KREY91, S. 159].

The correction factor in front of the root in equation (7.45) for various values of n is shown in Table 7.2.

Table 7.1 Gamma function values

x	0.5	1	1.5	2	2.5	3	3.5	4	4.5	5
$\Gamma(x)$	$\sqrt{\pi}$	1	$\frac{\sqrt{\pi}}{2}$	1	$\frac{3\cdot\sqrt{\pi}}{4}$	2	$\frac{15\cdot\sqrt{\pi}}{8}$	6	$\frac{105\cdot\sqrt{\pi}}{16}$	24
	1.7725	1.0000	0.8862	1.0000	1.3293	2.0000	3.3234	6.0000	11.631	24.000

Table 7.2 Correction factor values

n	2	3	4	5	6	7	8	9	10
$\dfrac{\Gamma\left(\frac{n-1}{2}\right)}{\Gamma\left(\frac{n}{2}\right)}$	1.7725	1.1284	0.8862	0.7523	0.6647	0.6018	0.5539	0.5158	0.4847

The values of a company for individual financial years (historical annual accounts and budgets) should likewise be calculated according to equation (7.42). The expositions given in the previous subsection apply regarding this. In relation to earlier annual accounts, we must — at this point — go particularly into years with negative free cash flows: it makes no sense to discount negative free cash flows. The reflection that every company disposes of a liquidation value, even if it may only be very small, is of further assistance here. From the point of view of the lending bank, the value of a company is never lower than the liquidation value that can be expected. This leads to the following equation for the value of a company, which must be substituted into equation (7.42):

$$V_k = \text{Max}\left(\frac{C_k}{i_{dk}}; V_{lk}\right) \tag{7.46}$$

If necessary, equation (7.46) for V should also be used in equation (7.44), especially in cases of winding up and reconstruction. The credit-worthiness and financial standing of any company in fact depend, strictly speaking, more than anything on liquidation value (see also Section 7.6).

The Black/Scholes model assumes volatility is constant. Merton [MERT73] showed later that the Black/Scholes model may be applied as it were unchanged, if volatility is not constant but is known as a function of time. The only difference is the definition of σ^2 as the average over the remaining term T of the option:

$$\sigma^2(T) = T^{-1} \cdot \int_0^T \sigma^2(t)\,dt \tag{7.47}$$

It is thus sufficient, to be able to apply the method described here, to have an adequately accurate idea of σ^2 over the loan's term.

Determination of the relevant volatility plays a central part in the whole option theory. It has only been possible here to show a practical method that is effective in application. The difficulties in determining volatility can be seen in, for example [SWD192], [RSS093], [KAR093], [HULL97, S. 499 and thereafter], [BCCH97] and [RITR98].

7.4.3 Private Debtors

The situation as regards private debtors can be shown by analogy with that of companies. With private debtors free cash flow is the equivalent of discretionary income after deduction of essential living costs. The more luxuries come to be regarded as necessities the smaller the borrowing power of the private individual becomes, and vice versa. For this reason, determining the correct figure to put on discretionary income at any one time, by talking to each individual borrower, is a tricky task for bankers.

Next we have to determine the appropriate discount rate i_d, with which the quasi-market value of the individual is found out. The CAPM may not be applied here, but the following reflection helps further, namely that the capability, in the case of the individual, to make interest payments and repayments, is of decisive importance. It is therefore appropriate to apply the highest possible loan interest rate that could be expected, taking into consideration any possible repayments, for the purposes of discounting. In the case of consumer credit, this is normally the legal interest rate cap. If the method outlined here ends up with a loan interest rate that is higher than the legal interest rate cap, then the business does not get done anyway.

By contrast with companies, two further risks have to be assessed in connection with an individual's discretionary income: the risks of death (and incapacity to work) and of unemployment. The former risk may be covered by the insurance industry on attractive terms. So in granting credit to individuals it is extremely important to take out appropriate insurance and to ensure the proceeds of it are assigned in favour of the bank.

The risk that the borrower may become unemployed must be taken into account by an adjustment to the figure for discretionary income. First the rate of unemployment benefit applicable, on the basis of the borrower's personal data in respect of age, occupation and residence, must be determined. Then the figure for discretionary income must be multiplied by a factor of 1 less the above-determined unemployment benefit, such that one obtains the expectation value of the discretionary income taking the risk of unemployment into account.

Once discretionary income for a few years back has been determined in this way — and used as a budget for the future — these values may be used instead of the free cash flows in the formulae described above. In this way loans to individuals also become assessable.

Only discretionary income has been taken into account in the reflections outlined here — any assets that may exist have not been considered. As no asset should be taken into account, by way of precaution, unless it is assigned in favour of the loan, the rules for covered loans apply, and these will be described in Chapters 8 and 9.

7.5 INFLUENCE OF INDIVIDUAL PARAMETERS ON THE CREDIT SHORTFALL RISK

As was shown in the previous section, the credit shortfall risk according to our model depends on the following influence factors:

- The company's debt rate d
- The annual volatility of the company's value σ
- The loan's term in years t

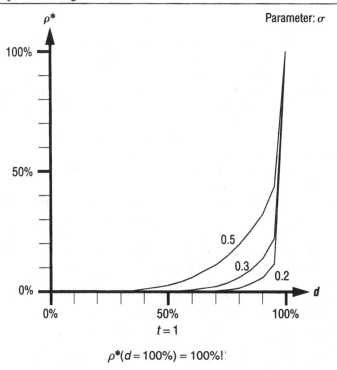

$$\rho^*(d = 100\%) = 100\%!$$

Figure 7.5

It is intended to demonstrate the influence of these parameters on the credit shortfall risk according to our model, with the help of the following diagrams.

Even though it has not been possible to date to carry out any costly empirical tests — for the reason that no bank in Switzerland has the necessary historically documented data available — the following diagrams do in fact line up qualitatively with the author's professional experience to date, which goes back at least 15 years.

Figure 7.5 shows that an appropriate credit shortfall risk switches in according to the volatility of the company's value, once a certain debt rate has been passed. It is important to note, at this point, that the following always applies:

$$\rho^*(d = 100\%) = 100\%!$$

If the loan granted is higher than the company's market value, then the risk exposure is 100%!

Figure 7.6 corresponds with Figure 7.5, but the credit shortfall risk axis has been spread out. Here it is evident that low credit shortfall risks result, even in the case of high debt rates, providing the volatility of the company's value is correspondingly low.

Figure 7.7 corresponds with Figure 7.6 to the extent that the debt rate axis has been spread out too. Here it is evident that low credit shortfall risks result, even in the case of very high debt rates such as those of banks and insurance companies, provided the volatility of the company's value is very low.

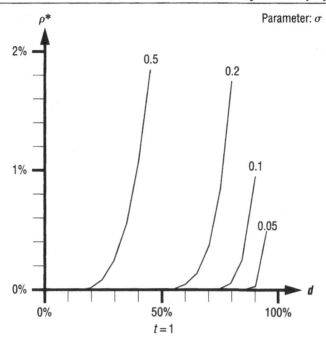

Figure 7.6

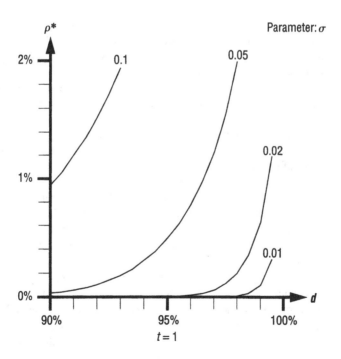

Figure 7.7

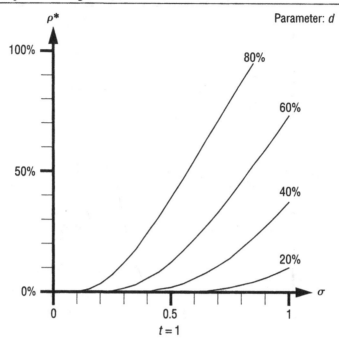

Figure 7.8

Figure 7.8 corresponds to Figure 7.5, but σ and d have been exchanged. Here it is evident that low credit shortfall risks result, even in the case of high volatility in company value, provided the debt rate is correspondingly low. Comparison between Figures 7.5 and 7.8 suggests the conclusion that more than anything else it is important for an entrepreneur to keep the volatility of the market value of his company low, and not necessarily its debt rate (compare comments in Section 9.4).

Figure 7.9 corresponds with Figure 7.8, with the credit shortfall risk axis again spread out. Here too it is evident that low credit shortfall risks result even in the case of high debt rates, provided the volatility of the value of the company is low.

Figure 7.10 demonstrates the course of the credit shortfall risk independently of the term of the loan and of the volatility of the company's value. The dependence of the credit-worthiness of a loan on the term of the loan with the same borrower, is clearly discernible.

Figure 7.11 corresponds to Figure 7.10, but over shorter loan terms.

Figure 7.12 corresponds to Figure 7.10, where the volatility of the company's value and its debt rate have changed places.

Figure 7.13 corresponds to Figure 7.12, but over shorter loan terms.

Figure 7.14 shows which pairs of values (σ, d) match the same credit shortfall risk. According to the guidelines of the rating agencies, a debtor receives a AAA/Aaa rating, if the shortfall risk amounts to less than one millionth over the whole term. The line with $\rho^*(t) = 1$ ppm therefore represents the AAA curve to the extent that all pairs of values below this curve match this top rating.

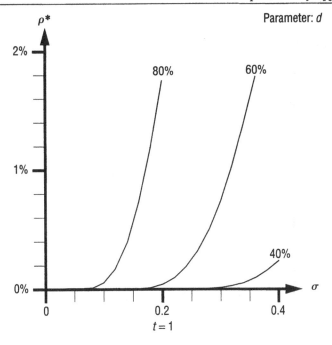

Figure 7.9

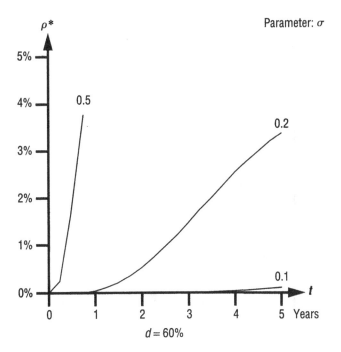

Figure 7.10

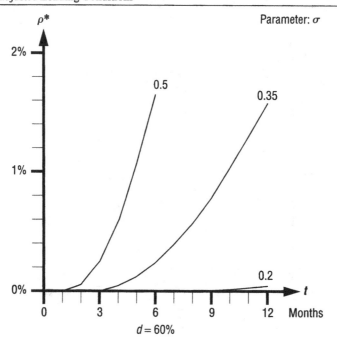

Figure 7.11

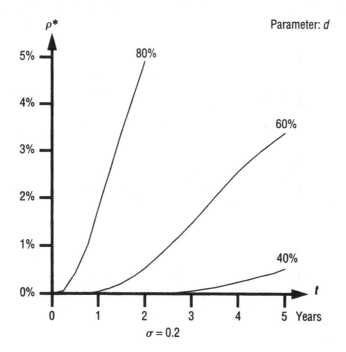

Figure 7.12

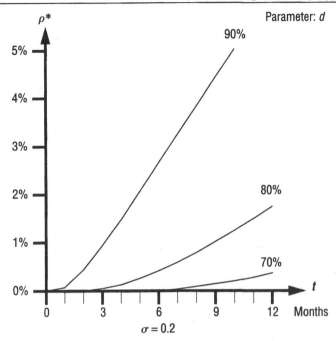

Figure 7.13

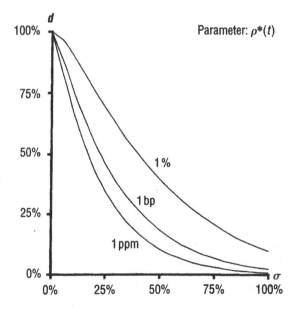

Figure 7.14

7.6   RISK OF BANKRUPTCY AND BREAKDOWN DISTRIBUTION

Up till now it has been the credit shortfall risk ρ^* that has been calculated. At this juncture we should demonstrate how the risk of a borrower's bankruptcy and the probably breakdown distributions may be calculated.

As may be inferred from Figure 7.3 in Section 7.2, the probability that a borrower is bankrupt at the time of the loan becoming due for repayment is none other than that of the put being in the money. This probability can be determined according to Cox and Rubinstein, with the notation introduced there [CORU85] being used in the paragraph printed in italics below, in order to be able to understand the derivation better.

The probability that a call is in the money at maturity amounts to $\Phi[a; n, p]$ [CORU85, S. 177], by using the complementary binomial distribution function. This probability receives the value $N(x - \sigma \cdot \sqrt{t})$ [CORU85, S. 208] in the case of transition to the standard normal distribution function. The probability of the corresponding put at maturity being in the money is therefore $1 - N(x - \sigma \cdot \sqrt{t})$ [CORU85, S. 4]. This becomes $N(x + \sigma \cdot \sqrt{t})$ on the basis of the symmetry properties of the standard normal distribution function [CORU85, S. 211].

Returning to the notation being used here, we can thus write, analogously, as follows:

$$\rho = N(x) \tag{7.48}$$

$$x = \frac{\ln\left(\frac{d}{1 - \rho^*}\right)}{\sigma \cdot \sqrt{t}} + \frac{\sigma \cdot \sqrt{t}}{2} \qquad \text{as per (7.38)}$$

With the credit shortfall risk ρ^* determined, the probability of bankruptcy ρ can thus also be determined. The breakdown distribution rate probability is calculated, according to equation (2.4) by

$$b = 1 - \frac{\rho^*}{\rho} = 1 - \frac{\rho^*}{N(x)} \tag{7.49}$$

and the expected breakdown distributions by:

$$B = b \cdot L \cdot (1 + i(t)) = \left(1 - \frac{\rho^*}{N(x)}\right) \cdot L \cdot (1 + i(t)) = \left(1 - \frac{\rho^*}{\rho}\right) \cdot L \cdot (1 + i(t)) \tag{7.50}$$

$i(t) =$ loan interest rate according to the whole term

As was emphasised at the end of Section 7.3, by way of qualification, the calculations in this chapter are based on the assumption that the loan interest for the whole term of the loan is due for payment only when the loan itself is due to be repaid. In the same way the calculation of the breakdown distribution rate is also based on this assumption, which should be taken into account here. In other words, the breakdown distribution rate relates to the nominal value of the loan plus all interest and compound interest over the whole term of the loan.

Let us remember, at this point, that the minimum market value of a company corresponds, according to equation (7.46) to its liquidation value. This leads to the following reflections:

- Companies of good financial standing have high revenues and thus high market values, which are always higher than the balance sheet figures produced by their accountants (and let us remember at this point, too, that it is the market value of the *debt-free* company that is used for risk calculation). Loans are thus small in size in relation to the company's market value. That leads to very low shortfall risks — in the main just theoretical.

- On the other hand companies of poor financial standing have low revenues and thus low market values. As soon as a serious crisis looms, it may thus be assumed that it is the liquidation value that is used, according to subsection 7.4.2, for the risk calculation, which lines up with banking practice. This may lead consequentially to an existing loan in this situation being called in, or to an application for a new loan not being followed up.

7.7 LOAN ASSESSMENT

The derivation of the risk-adjusted loan interest rate when extending credit having been analysed in Sections 7.3 to 7.6, this section will deal with assessing a loan that has already been granted during its term, in which on the basis of the loan agreement the loan interest rate up to the time the loan is due to be repaid can no longer be adjusted to be consistent with risk, although new information for assessing it is available. The basic equations from Section 7.2 again form the starting point for our considerations.

The value of a loan during its term can be calculated with the aid of equations (7.6) and (7.12), in which we must, however, distinguish between the market and the nominal value of the loan. This leads to the following equation, in which $(1 + i)/(1 + i_s) = 1/(1 - \rho^*)$ no longer applies, as the interest rate during the contractually agreed term of the loan may no longer be adjusted to be consistent with risk:

$$\Lambda = L \cdot \left(\frac{1 + i_{\text{pa}}}{1 + i_{\text{spa}}}\right)^t - L \cdot \left(\frac{1 + i_{\text{pa}}}{1 + i_{\text{spa}}}\right)^t \cdot N(x) + V \cdot N(x - \sigma \cdot \sqrt{t}) \qquad (7.51)$$

Summarised, this results in:

$$\Lambda = L \cdot \left(\frac{1 + i_{\text{pa}}}{1 + i_{\text{spa}}}\right)^t \cdot (1 - N(x)) + V \cdot N(x - \sigma \cdot \sqrt{t}) \qquad (7.52)$$

$$\text{with: } x = \frac{\ln\left(d \cdot \left(\frac{1 + i_{\text{pa}}}{1 + i_{\text{spa}}}\right)^t\right)}{\sigma \cdot \sqrt{t}} + \frac{\sigma \cdot \sqrt{t}}{2} \qquad (7.53)$$

In this, t means the rest of the loan's term and the interest rates i_{pa} and i_{spa} and the volatility σ must be inserted on an annual basis. Moreover, the current standard rate of interest appropriate to the remainder of the term must be used for i_{spa}. As will be evident from equations (7.48)–(7.49), $\Lambda = L$, if i_{pa} according to ρ^* is consistent with risk!

Unlike Section 7.3, where in the risk-adjusted case for $d > 1$ there is no longer any solution for ρ^* (or where $\rho^* = 100\%$) (cf. notes on Figure 7.5), there is a solution here for all values of d. This is explained by the fact that it is indeed normal that conditions may no longer be adjusted to be consistent with risk in new circumstances during the agreed fixed term of the loan. This gives expression to the fact that it is only the situation when the loan is due for repayment that is decisive. Even if the value of d is greater than 1 during the term, the market value of the company through to the end of the term may improve again, and the situation of d being less than 1 may be achieved again by the time the loan is due for repayment. Expressed in terms of option theory: even if the put during the loan's term is occasionally in the money, that does not necessarily mean that it is also in the money at maturity (compare also with Brealey and Myers [BRMY96, S. 564]).

For the case in which the liabilities side is made up of several loans, the debts as a whole must be inserted for L and assessed according to the remaining term of the loan in question. The value of the loan being considered then works out in proportion to its share of the debts. Here the values of the loan under consideration must be used for the rates of interest i_{pa} and i_{spa}. Tackled this way we can be certain that the loan in question is assessed according to its characteristics, but taking into account the total of debt (see also Section 8.4).

7.8   BONDS

Bonds can be assessed in exactly the same way as bank loans, according to Section 7.7. With the help of equations (7.52)–(7.53), however, the converse, namely the volatility implicit in the stock exchange, may be calculated on the basis of the stock exchange price.

With the aid of volatility investigated in this way, the shortfall risk implicit in the stock exchange, and therefore the bond's rating, may be determined using equations (7.37)–(7.38).

7.9   CONSIDERATION OF PRIVILEGED SALARY CLAIMS IN THE EVENT OF BANKRUPTCY

The salary claims of a company's workforce are privileged in the case of bankruptcy, under Swiss debt recovery and bankruptcy law. Under this the date on which bankruptcy proceedings are commenced is taken as the date on which notice of termination of employment is given. The privileged demand of each person employed is that person's salary claim up until the expiry of the notice period according to his/her contract of employment. In contrast to all other relevant liabilities in bankruptcy, the company does not have to account for these salary claims prior to bankruptcy. These salary claims have thus not been taken into account in the considerations in this chapter so far. This shall now be remedied.

Under equation (7.50) the breakdown distribution probability value comes to:

$$B = b \cdot L \cdot (1 + i(t)) = \left(1 - \frac{\rho^*}{\rho}\right) \cdot L \cdot (1 + i(t)) \tag{7.50}$$

First of all the privileged salary claims have now to be deducted from the expectation value of the breakdown distribution available for distribution:

$$B_c = b \cdot L \cdot (1 + i(t)) - S = \left(1 - \frac{\rho^*}{\rho}\right) \cdot L \cdot (1 + i(t)) - S \tag{7.54}$$

B_c = corrected breakdown distribution
S = proportional salaries

It should be noted that, in the case of several loans, only the proportional salaries have to be taken into account for any individual loan that has to be assessed. This implies the following: in bankruptcy the whole amount for salaries is deducted from the overall breakdown distribution.

The rest is distributed proportionately across the individual loan demands. From the point of view of the individual lender, however, this means nothing more than that it has to make a proportionate contribution to the privileged salary claims that have to be met, from the breakdown distributions that were 'originally' available to it.

The percentage rate of the salary total falling against it in this way corresponds to percentage figure of its loan claim in relation to the total loan.

It is quite possible that the salary claims in bankruptcy are higher than the probable break-down distributions. Thus a negative figure for corrected probable breakdown distributions would result, which would make no sense. This just means that the salary claims are no longer covered at all. Equation (7.50) must therefore be correctly written as follows:

$$B_c = \text{Max}(b \cdot L \cdot (1 + i(t)) - S; 0) \tag{7.55}$$

Continuing, the corrected breakdown distribution rate probability can be detailed as follows:

$$b_c = \frac{B_c}{L \cdot (1 + i_c(t))} = \frac{\text{Max}(b \cdot L \cdot (1 + i(t)) - S; 0)}{L \cdot (1 + i_c(t))} \tag{7.56}$$

b_c = corrected breakdown distribution rate
$i_c(t)$ = corrected loan interest rate according to the whole term

It is essential at this point to note the distinction between $i(t)$ and $i_c(t)$! $i(t)$ concerns the uncorrected rate of interest that has already been calculated, while $i_c(t)$ concerns the corrected value still to be calculated.

The corrected credit risk can now be calculated with the aid of equation (2.6):

$$\rho_c^* = \rho \cdot (1 - b_c) = \rho \cdot \left(1 - \frac{\text{Max}(b \cdot L \cdot (1 + i(t)); 0)}{L \cdot (1 + i_c(t))}\right) \tag{7.57}$$

ρ_c^* = corrected credit risk

For the case where $b_c = 0$, the solution is:

$$\rho_c^* = \rho \quad \text{if } b_c = 0 \tag{7.58}$$

For other cases the following applies:

$$\rho_c^* = \rho \cdot (1 - b_c) = \rho \cdot \left(1 - \frac{B_c}{L \cdot (1 + i_c(t))}\right) \tag{7.59}$$

On the other hand, the corrected credit risk may be calculated by:

$$i_c(t) = \frac{i_s + \rho_c^*}{1 - \rho_c^*} = \frac{i_s + \rho \cdot (1 - b_c)}{1 - \rho \cdot (1 - b_c)} \tag{7.60}$$

Both equations (7.59) and (7.60) now permit calculation of the corrected breakdown distri-bution rate probability b_c. The middle and right-hand term of equation (7.59) are used. Cancel out with ρ, subtract from 1 and cancel out by -1 results in:

$$b_c = \frac{B_c}{L \cdot (1 + i_c(t))} = \frac{B_c}{L \cdot \left(1 + \frac{i_s(t) + \rho \cdot (1 - b_c)}{1 - \rho \cdot (1 - b_c)}\right)} \tag{7.61}$$

Transformation of the denominator in the right-hand term of equation (7.61) gives:

$$b_c = \frac{B_c}{L \cdot \frac{(1+i_s(t))}{(1-\rho \cdot (1-b_c))}} = \frac{B_c \cdot (1 - \rho \cdot (1 - b_c))}{L \cdot (1 + i_s(t))} \qquad (7.62)$$

Reduce to the lowest common denominator using the denominator in the right-hand term of equation (7.62) and multiply out gives:

$$b_c \cdot L \cdot (1 + i_s) = B_c - \rho \cdot B_c + \rho \cdot B_c \cdot b_c \qquad (7.63)$$

Solving by b_c leads to:

$$b_c = \frac{B_c \cdot (1 - \rho)}{L \cdot (1 + i_s(t)) - B_c \cdot \rho} \qquad (7.64)$$

The corrected credit shortfall risk is thus:

$$\rho_c^* = \rho \cdot (1 - b_c) = \rho \cdot \left(1 - \frac{B_c \cdot (1 - \rho)}{L \cdot (1 + i_s(t)) - B_c \cdot \rho} \right) \qquad (7.65)$$

This credit has still to be converted on an annual basis according to equation (7.39).

7.10   LIMITS TO THE APPLICATION OF THE OPTION THEORY APPROACH

The preconditions that have to be fulfilled in order to be able to apply the Black and Scholes model are specified in Cox and Rubinstein [CORU85, S. 268]. They are explained below, with the terms having been 'translated' for the application described here.

1. **The company does not make any distribution payments (dividends and interest) during the period under consideration.**
   The method described here takes the free cash flows of the debt-free imaginary company as the basis for assessing its credit-worthiness. The assessment rests thus on the amount of revenue *before* interest and dividends. In the assessment this figure is determined for each financial year being taken into consideration, independently of the other financial years. The distributions of dividends and payment of interest thus do not have any influence on the assessment in the method described here, as long as the approved and calculated loans are not changed (raised) as a result of the payment of dividends and interest.
2. **Notice to terminate the loan may only be given at the end of the period under consideration.**
   This precondition is always fulfilled.
3. **There are no requirements in terms of margins, taxation or transaction expenses.**
   This precondition is fulfilled as it is just a question, in the case of the put in the application described here, of a theoretical construction and not of anything existing in real life.
4. **The level of interest is constant.**
   As was shown in this chapter, the credit-worthiness of a company is on the one hand independent of the interest level; in contrast to the solution as it was indicated in Cox and

Rubinstein [CORU85, S. 382] (see Section 7.1). The assessment of the market risk on the other hand was intentionally excluded here (see Section 1.2).

5. **The volatility of the company's value is constant.**
   The approach described here may only be applied if reliable assumptions are made about future volatility. Only the calculating out of various scenarios can show whether or not the uncertainties are decisive in terms of price. In so far as this is the case, the appropriate consequences have to be drawn; either the price has to be set in line with the worst-case scenario, or no loan must be made at all. The precondition of constant volatility was qualified by Merton [MERT 73], as we have already mentioned: compare also subsection 7.4.2 with the reading references given there. It must not, however, be denied that volatility represents the crux of all applications of option price models. Even Cox and Rubinstein write [in CORU85, S. 258] that 'the critical feature for option pricing is the behaviour of the volatility'.

6. **Only very small changes in the valuation of a company can occur in very short periods of time.**
   This precondition may usually be regarded as fulfilled. Major changes are often attributable to errors in earlier assessments and are therefore artificial. In any such case the errors should be corrected and the assessment undertaken afresh.
   A further precondition is mentioned in Cox and Rubinstein [CORU85, S. 276].

7. **Changes in the value of a company must be distributed lognormally.**
   There are statistical tests to check whether any existing frequency distribution out of n observations (here: appraised company accounts and budgets), that has been obtained as a result of a random sample, is consistent with a hypothesis that has been drawn on distribution in the parent population (here: lognormal distribution), and these tests are described in the reading (for example, BOHL92, S. 625 and thereafter). Because of the statistically small volumes of data in the form of appraised company accounts and budgets, use of the visual test by means of a probability paper (for example, BOHL92, S. 625 and thereafter) is recommended — it being possible these days to run this up on to a screen with the help of the computer [BOHL92, S. 629].

   The further back a company's track record goes, the more precisely can it normally be established whether or not the condition is fulfilled. One qualification results from the point that track records may only be used as far back as there may not have occurred, in the period concerned, any substantial events changing the nature of the company. By this we mean events such as mergers, divestments, major changes in commercial strategies and so on.

   Kremer and Roenfeldt [KRRO92] moreover pose the question of whether the Black and Scholes model is usable at all for longer-term examinations. They argue that officially quoted options have a maximum term of 270 days. The Black/Scholes assumption within this time scale, in which the value of the asset base is changing continually but only in small steps, may well be permissible, but not over longer examination time scales. In their article about warrants, they conclude that their 'jump-diffusion' model in the case of warrants exerciseable in more than one year (for out of money warrants) may deliver more reliable results than the Black and Scholes model. Translated into extending credit, this means a loan assessment endures only so long as the company laying claim to it is not subject to any substantial changes of the kind mentioned above. The requirement that loan agreement clauses must contain appropriate passages follows on from this. Even for long-term loans, such as fixed-date mortgage loans over several years, it must thus be possible, if important events defined in advance (see above) occur, to adjust the loan conditions to new circumstances.

A further qualification emerges on the point of the extent to which information exists at all. A company must after all have a 'track record' in the first place, for an assessment of it to be possible. This, however, is of course not the case with recently founded enterprises. The only way forward in this situation is to work on the basis of budgets. Here the risk must be checked, with the aid of model calculations and the help of specimen scenarios, to see whether it can be circumscribed with sufficient precision, or the company applying for the loan must be prepared to pay interest on a worst-case scenario basis.

7.11   RESULTS AND CONCLUSIONS

A company's credit shortfall risk can be calculated using equations (7.37)–(7.38), independently of the risk-free rate of interest:

$$\rho^*(t) = \frac{N(x - \sigma \cdot \sqrt{t}) - d \cdot N(x)}{N(x - \sigma \cdot \sqrt{t}) - d} \tag{7.37}$$

$$\text{with: } x = \frac{\ln\left(\frac{d}{1-\rho^*(t)}\right)}{\sigma \cdot \sqrt{t}} + \frac{\sigma \cdot \sqrt{t}}{2} \tag{7.38}$$

As $\rho^*(t)$ in the above equations corresponds to the credit shortfall risk over the whole term of the loan, the value should be calculated on an annual basis:

$$\rho^*_{\text{pa}} = 1 - \sqrt[t]{1 - \rho^*(t)} \tag{7.39}$$

The risk-adjusted loan interest rate per annum is then calculated from that, as follows:

$$i_{\text{pa}} = \frac{i_{\text{spa}} + \rho^*_{\text{pa}}}{1 - \rho^*_{\text{pa}}} \tag{7.40}$$

A loan that has already been granted may be continually assessed for risk-adjustment right through to its maturity. Assessment is made in the case of t years according to the equations:

$$\Lambda(t) = L \cdot \left(\frac{1 + i_{\text{pa}}}{1 + i_{\text{spa}}}\right)^t \cdot (1 - N(x)) + V \cdot N(x - \sigma \cdot \sqrt{t}) \tag{7.52}$$

$$\text{with: } x = \frac{\ln\left(d \cdot \left(\frac{1 + i_{\text{pa}}}{1 + i_{\text{spa}}}\right)^t\right)}{\sigma\sqrt{t}} + \frac{\sigma \cdot \sqrt{t}}{2} \tag{7.53}$$

The risk-adjusted loan interest rate can also take privileged salary claims into account in the event of bankruptcy: first the corrected expectation value of breakdown distributions is calculated:

$$B_c = \text{Max} \cdot (b \cdot L \cdot (1 + i(t)) - S; 0) \qquad (7.55)$$

The corrected credit shortfall risk may then be calculated:

$$\rho_c^* = \rho \cdot \left(1 - \frac{B_c \cdot (1 - \rho)}{L \cdot (1 + i_s(t)) - B_c \cdot \rho}\right) \qquad (7.65)$$

This value must then be converted again according to equation (7.39). The loan interest rate also ensues from equation (7.40). An Excel worksheet is presented in Appendix 2 with which the equations specified above may be applied.

7.12 EXAMPLES

The method outlined here is explained with the aid of two examples.

7.12.1 Example of a Company with Continuous Business Development

The key figures needed for the model are given in Table 7.3.

The liquidation value is lower in all years than the discounted free cash flows, which is why this applies as the company's value, according to equation (7.46).

Debts are summarised together as follows:

Creditors	50
1-year loan(s)	500
3-year loan(s)	1000
Total debts	1550

Debt rate: $1550/2500 = 62\%$

The natural logarithms must first be calculated according to equation (7.42) for the calculation of volatility:

Table 7.3 Key figures — Example 1

Year	−3	−2	−1	0	+1 (Budget)
Turnover	1000	1025	1100	1150	1250
Operating costs	700	750	800	850	900
Capital investments	100	110	100	90	100
Free cash flow	200	165	200	210	250
Discount rate	10%	10%	10%	10%	10%
Discounted free cash flows	2000	1650	2000	2100	2500
Liquidation value	1000	1000	1000	1000	1000
Value of company	2000	1650	2000	2100	2500

Table 7.4 Shortfall risks in Example 1

	$\sigma\sqrt{t}$	x	$N(x)$	$N(x - \sigma\sqrt{t})$	ρ^*
1 year	19.25%	−2.3844	0.0086	0.0050	0.0518%
3 years	33.34%	−1.2195	0.1113	0.0602	1.5724%

Table 7.5 Final results of Example 1

	Rating	ρ_{pa}^* according to rating	i_s (assumption)	i according to equation (4.49)	i rounded up
1 year	AA	0.0733%	4.0%	4.0763%	$4\frac{1}{8}\%$
3 years	BB	0.7570%	4.5%	5.2971%	$5\frac{5}{16}\%$

Table 7.6 Bankruptcy situation in Example 1

	ρ^*	ρ	b	$L(1 + i(t))$	B
1 year	0.0518%	0.8554%	93.94%	520	489
3 years	1.5724%	11.1329%	85.88%	1159	996

$$\ln(1650/2000) = -0.1924$$
$$\ln(2000/1650) = 0.1924$$
$$\ln(2100/2000) = 0.0488$$
$$\ln(2500/2100) = 0.1744$$
$$\text{mean } \mu = 0.0558$$

Using equation (7.45) a volatility of $\sigma = 19.25\%$ results from this.

The iterative calculation delivers the results shown in Table 7.4, using an Excel worksheet.

The result for ρ^* must now be converted to one year, according to the rules for transforming time periods (equation (7.39)):

1 year: $\rho_{pa}^* = 0.0518\%$
3 years: $\rho_{pa}^* = 0.5269\%$

The one-year loan receives an AA rating and the three-year loan receives a BB rating according to Table 2.1. This leads to the final results for the loan rates of interest consistent with risk, according to Table 7.5. It is striking that despite the relatively small volatility of not quite 20% and a debt rate of almost two-thirds, there is a considerable difference in interest between the one-year and the three-year loan.

The situation that may now be expected in any possible case of bankruptcy may be calculated, using equations (7.48, 7.49 and 7.50) and shown in Table 7.6.

Table 7.7   Proportion of privileged salary claims

Liabilities	Amount	Share of salary claims
Creditors	50	2
Loan 1 Year	500	20
Loan 3 Years	1000	40
Total	1550	62

Table 7.8   Final results after privileged salary claims

	B_c	$b_c(\%)$	$\rho_c^*(\%)$	$\rho_{cpa}^*(\%)$	Rating	i_s (assumption)	i according to (4.49)	i rounded up
1 year	469	90.12	0.849	0.849	A	4.0%	4.1780%	$4\frac{3}{16}\%$
3 years	956	82.07	1.9959	0.6698	BB	4.5%	5.2971%	$5\frac{5}{16}\%$

If the entrepreneur gives up his company after one year, the bank may thus assume that the loans, including accumulated interest over the whole terms of them, still have a value of about 94% and after three years a value of about 86%. (Here the interest must be calculated precisely using the values of ρ^* given in Table 7.4.)

It is now our intention to investigate, in the event of bankruptcy according to Section 7.9, what effect the salary claims have on the credit risk. The salary and wage claims to be expected in the event of bankruptcy are 62. They spread out over the liabilities, as in Section 7.9, as shown in Table 7.7.

This leads, using equations (7.55), (7.64) and (7.65) together with the values from Table 7.7, to the corrected credit shortfall risks, ratings and loan interest rates shown in Table 7.8.

Taking the salary claims in the event of bankruptcy into account in the case of the one-year loan has led to deterioration in the credit-worthiness by one rating level. The rating level has not deteriorated in the case of the three-year loan, despite an increase in risk. This comes about because the 'higher' rating levels are 'broader' than the 'lower' rating levels, and because the values in the case concerned are correspondingly favourable.

7.12.2   Example of a Company with a Poor Financial Year

The key figures needed are again given in Table 7.9.

In year −1 the liquidation value is higher than the discounted free cash flows, which is why this value is put in as the company's value. Debts are summarised together as follows:

Creditors	50
1-year loan(s)	500
3-year loan(s)	500
Total debts	1050

Table 7.9   Starting position Example 2

Year	−3	−2	−1	0	+1 (Budget)
Turnover	1000	1025	1100	1150	1200
Operating costs	700	750	800	850	900
Capital investments	100	120	50	100	100
Free cash flow	200	230	50	100	200
Discount rate	10%	10%	10%	10%	10%
Discounted free cash flows	2000	2300	500	1000	2000
Liquidation value	1000	1000	1000	1000	1000
Value of company	2000	2300	1000	1100	2000

Table 7.10   Shortfall risks in Example 2

	$\sigma\sqrt{t}$	x	$N(x)$	$N\cdot(x-\sigma\sqrt{t})$	ρ^*
1 year	68.47%	−0.4307	0.3333	0.1323	10.8658%
3 years	118.59%	0.5070	0.6939	0.2486	41.8652%

Debt rate: $1050/2500 = 52.5\%$

The volatility calculation is made analogously to the previous example:

$\ln(2300/2000) = 0.1398$
$\ln(1000/2300) = -0.8329$
$\ln(1000/1000) = 0.0000$
$\ln(2000/1000) = 0.6931$
$\quad$ mean $\mu = 0.0000$

That results in a volatility of 68.47% according to equation (7.45). The iterative calculation delivers the results shown in Table 7.10, using an Excel worksheet.

The transformation of time periods according to equation (7.39) gives the following results:

1 year: $\quad \rho^*_{pa} = 10.87\%$
3 years: $\quad \rho^*_{pa} = 16.54\%$

Using Table 2.1, this leads to the ratings and final results for the loan rates of interest consistent with risk shown in Table 7.11.

The poor financial year − 1 has increased the volatility of the company's value markedly. The loan rates of interest consistent with risk are substantially higher than in the previous example, despite the clearly lower debt.

Table 7.11 Final results of Example 2

	Rating	ρ_{pa}^* according to rating	i_s (assumption)	i according to equation (4.49)	i rounded up
1 year	C	12.4786%	4.0%	18.8281%	$18\frac{7}{8}\%$
3 years	DDD	24.9871%	4.5%	39.2993%	$39\frac{5}{16}\%$

Table 7.12 Bankruptcy situation in Example 2

	ρ^*	ρ	b	$L(1+i(t))$	B
1 year	10.87%	33.33%	67.40%	583	393
3 years	41.87%	69.39%	39.67%	981	389

The situation shown in Table 7.12 is to be expected in any possible event of bankruptcy.

Taking the salary claims in the event of bankruptcy into account by analogy with the previous example is left to the reader.

Comparison of the results of the two examples in subsections 7.12.1 and 7.12.2 permits the supposition that in today's banking practice, in cases of companies having had poor financial years in the recent past and whose values are therefore highly volatile, loan interest rates have been allowed to apply that are much too low.

8
Loans Covered against Shortfall Risk

In this chapter we will examine the shortfall risk of covered loans, where the bank in principle relies exclusively on the collateral. As was illustrated in the comments on Figure 7.5, no loan may ever be greater, at the time of its being issued, than the market value of the company or the equivalent of that in respect of the private individual. The same applies, analogously, for loans that are covered, but on which the bank relies on the collateral alone: the loan may not be higher than the value of the collateral, so long as it is geared to the collateral alone. The smaller the loan in relation to the value of the collateral, the smaller is the risk on the loan, and vice versa. This fact is probed in Section 8.1.

In Sections 8.2 and 8.3 we will, in passing, relax this assumption, in that in the case of the collateral falling short the loan will not necessarily be in default as long as the borrower is still in a position to service it. This way of looking at it rests on the assumption that banks usually only make loans when borrowers are, to all intents and purposes, in a position to service them without any difficulty. Collateral here only serves the bank as guarantee against the case that is out of the ordinary. In Section 8.2 the correlation between the probabilities of the collateral falling short and of the borrower defaulting will first be examined. The results of Sections 8.1 and 8.2 will be summarised in Section 8.3.

How to proceed in the case of a combination of one covered loan and one uncovered loan to the same borrower will be investigated in Section 8.4. Here only the fact that one loan is covered, and the other not, will be taken into account, with the consequences which ensue from that fact. The question of the optimum combination of covered and uncovered loans, and thus also the question of a loan that is partially covered, will not be investigated until Chapter 9.

The results of this chapter will be illustrated in Section 8.6 by means of an example.

8.1 SHORTFALL RISK OF A COVERED LOAN ON THE BASIS OF THE OPTION-THEORY APPROACH

A covered loan, where the bank is relying exclusively on the cover, is in default if the value of the collateral no longer matches the mortgaging bank's minimum claim. This consideration leads to the same result for the company as in Chapter 7, with terms being substituted as shown in Table 8.1.

In the case of covered loans the time from the completion of the loan to the realisation of the collateral must also be taken into account in the bank's reaction time. Experience shows that this can take from just a few days in the case of securities offered as collateral, to several years in the case of mortgages.

In the case of securities it is possible to reassess the collateral daily, and electronically, on the basis of stock exchange data. More information is thus available for the calculation of

Table 8.1   Uncovered versus covered loans

Variable	Chapter 7	Chapter 8
V	Market value of the company	Value of collateral
D, L	Debts	Mortgage
E	Equity	Unmortgaged portion of collateral
σ	Volatility of the value of the company	Volatility of the value of the collateral
d	Debt rate	Mortgage rate
t	(Remaining)term of loan and/or reaction time in the case of current account lending	(Remaining)term of loan and/or reaction time in the case of current account lending and variable mortgages

volatility in the case of securities used as collateral, which leads to a simplification *vis-à-vis* equation (7.27) [CORU85, S. 256]:

$$\sigma = \sqrt{\frac{A}{n-1} \cdot \sum_{k=1}^{n} \left(\ln \left(\frac{X_k}{X_k - 1} \right) - \mu \right)^2}$$ (8.1)

$$\text{with } \mu = \frac{1}{n} \cdot \sum_{k=1}^{n} \ln \left(\frac{X_k}{X_k - 1} \right)$$

$X = $ portfolio values
$A = $ number of trading days per year

In order to be able to assess mortgage loans, the current value of the property concerned must be known, together with the volatility of this value. The determination of the current value of a property is common practice for any bank. It cannot actually be said that this is free of problems, but they are known and largely under control.

It is more difficult with the determination of volatility. For this not only the current value of any property but also the probable development in its value has to be known. Credit is due to the Cantonal Bank of Zürich's pioneering work in this field, whereby it developed a property price index based on the 'hedonistic' method. This method not only allows for the published index to be drawn up, but also makes it possible for an individual calculation of the probable development in the value of any property to be drawn up. See [ZKB96] for details. Index valuations may be downloaded from the Internet (see Appendix 3).

The loan risk of the covered loan is calculated using equations (7.37)–(7.38), the shortfall risk of the collateral using equation (7.48) and the breakdown distribution probability value using equation (7.49). It is important to distinguish clearly between these values. They are therefore detailed once more at this juncture:

$$p_C^* = \frac{N_C(x_C - \sigma_C \cdot \sqrt{t}) - d_C \cdot N_C(x_C)}{N_C(x_C - \sigma_C \cdot \sqrt{t}) - d_C}$$ (7.37)

$$\text{with } x = \frac{\ln\left(\frac{d}{1-\rho^*}\right)}{\sigma \cdot \sqrt{t}} + \frac{\sigma \cdot \sqrt{t}}{2} \tag{7.38}$$

$$\rho_C = N_C(x_C) \tag{7.47}$$

$$b_C = 1 - \frac{\rho_C^*}{\rho_C} = \frac{\rho_C^*}{N_C(x_C)} \tag{7.48}$$

Index C = collateral

8.2 CORRELATION BETWEEN THE SHORTFALL RISK OF THE BORROWER AND THE SHORTFALL RISK OF THE COLLATERAL

If a covered loan defaults only on account of the collateral, that does not necessarily mean that the loan is effectively lost to the bank. The borrower may indeed be in as good a position as previously to meet its obligations to the bank on the strength of its solvency. It is still of course just as much as before the bank's contractual partner. This section will therefore deal with determining the combined shortfall risk of the borrower and of the collateral, taking the correlation between the two into account.

8.2.1 Derivation of the Correlation

The probabilities of four possible occurrences within a period of time have to be considered in the case of a covered loan:

- Probability $\hat{a}$, that both the borrower defaults and the collateral falls short.
- Probability $\hat{b}$, that neither the borrower defaults nor the collateral falls short.
- Probability $\hat{c}$, that only the collateral falls short, but that the borrower does not default.
- Probability $\hat{d}$, that the borrower defaults, but that the collateral does not fall short.

This can be illustrated graphically as shown in Figure 8.1.

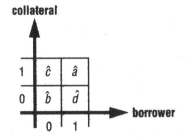

The 'default' occurrence has a value of '1'.

The 'no default' occurrence has a value of '0'.

Figure 8.1

The following correlations are discernible on the basis of Figure 8.1.

$$\rho_{B \cap C} = \hat{a}$$
$$\rho_B = \hat{a} + \hat{d}$$
$$\rho_C = \hat{a} + \hat{c}$$
$$1 = \hat{a} + \hat{b} + \hat{c} + \hat{d}$$

(8.2)

$\rho_{B \cap C} =$ combined risk
Index $B =$ borrower

One obtains the following [KREY91, S. 304] for the correlation of this frequency distribution:

$$\hat{r} = \frac{\hat{a} - (\hat{a} + \hat{d}) \cdot (\hat{a} + \hat{c})}{\sqrt{[(\hat{a} + \hat{d}) - (\hat{a} + \hat{d})^2] \cdot [(\hat{a} + \hat{c}) - (\hat{a} + \hat{c})^2]}}$$

(8.3)

$\hat{r} =$ correlation coefficient

After insertion of the shortfall risks according to equation (8.2), one obtains:

$$\hat{r} = \frac{\rho_{B \cap C} - \rho_B \cdot \rho_C}{\sqrt{[\rho_B - \rho_B^2] \cdot [\rho_C - \rho_C^2]}}$$

(8.4)

Solution using $\rho_{B \cap C}$ results in:

$$\rho_{B \cap C} = \rho_B \cdot \rho_C + \hat{r} \cdot \sqrt{\left(\rho_B - \rho_B^2\right) \cdot \left(\rho_C - \rho_C^2\right)}$$

(8.5)

It is then possible to calculate the combined shortfall risk, provided the individual shortfall risks and the correlation coefficient are known. In the special case $\hat{r} = 0$, i.e. in which there is no correlation at all, equation (8.5) reduces itself to $\rho_{B \cap C} = \rho_B \cdot \rho_C$, as one would expect according to the multiplication rules that apply to the probability of independent occurrences [BOHL92, S. 324].

8.2.2   Value Area of the Efficiency of the Correlation

It is intended next to investigate what values may theoretically be assumed for $\hat{r}$ and $\rho_{B \cap C}$.

Minimum

First of all the minimum should be calculated. The frequency distribution may then be portrayed as follows and shown graphically in Figure 8.2, whereby this involves a theoretically conceivable perfect hedge that is, however, unrealistic in practice.

$$\rho_{B \cap C} = 0$$
$$\rho_B = \hat{d}$$
$$\rho_C = \hat{c}$$
$$1 = \hat{b} + \hat{c} + \hat{d}$$

(8.6)

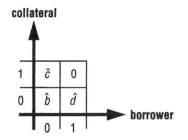

The 'default' occurrence has a value of '1'.

The 'no default' occurrence has a value of '0'.

Figure 8.2

One obtains the following [KREY91, S. 304] for the correlation of this frequency distribution:

$$\hat{r} = \frac{0 - \hat{d} \cdot \hat{c}}{\sqrt{(\hat{d} - \hat{d}^2) \cdot (\hat{c} - \hat{c}^2)}} \tag{8.7}$$

After insertion of the shortfall risks according to equation (8.6), one obtains:

$$\hat{r}_{\min} = \frac{-\rho_B \cdot \rho_C}{\sqrt{\left(\rho_B - \rho_B^2\right) \cdot \left(\rho_C - \rho^2 C\right)}} \tag{8.8}$$

According to statistical theory, the lowest value that a correlation coefficient may assume is -1 [BOHL92, S.235]. We now intend to investigate under what assumptions this value may be reached.

$$-1 = \frac{-\rho_B \cdot \rho_C}{\sqrt{\left(\rho_B - \rho_B^2\right) \cdot \left(\rho_C - \rho_C^2\right)}} \tag{8.9}$$

Conversion results in:

$$\left(\rho_B - \rho_B^2\right) \cdot \left(\rho_C - \rho_C^2\right) = \rho_B^2 \cdot \rho_C^2 \tag{8.10}$$

Multiplying out gives:

$$\rho_B \cdot \rho_C - \left(\rho_B \cdot \rho_C^2 + \rho_C \cdot \rho_B^2\right) + \rho_B^2 \cdot \rho_C^2 = \rho_B^2 \cdot \rho_C^2 \tag{8.11}$$

Which leads to:

$$1 = \rho_B + \rho_C \tag{8.12}$$

$\hat{r}$ may thus only assume the value -1 if the sum of both individual risks is equal to 1. This means, on the basis of equation (8.6), that $\hat{b} = 0$ in this case.

Maximum

Maximum values for $\hat{r}$ and $\rho_{B \cap C}$ are reached by the consideration that such is the case if collateral falling short leads to default on the loan, i.e. $\rho_{B \cap C} = \rho_C$. The frequency distribution

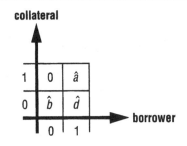

collateral

The 'default' occurrence has a value of '1'.

The 'no default' occurrence has a value of '0'.

Figure 8.3

can then be portrayed as follows and illustrated in Figure 8.3.

$$\begin{aligned}
\rho_{B \cap C} &= \hat{a} \\
\rho_B &= \hat{a} + \hat{d} \\
\rho_C &= \hat{a} \\
1 &= \hat{a} + \hat{b} + \hat{d}
\end{aligned}$$
(8.13)

As $\hat{d} \geq 0$ applies as probability value for $\hat{d}$, this means that $\rho_B \geq \rho_C$. The shortfall risk of the borrower is thus greater or at least equal to the shortfall risk of the collateral and to the combined shortfall risk respectively. This makes sense, as the bank would of course not otherwise fall back on collateral at the time of granting the loan. One obtains the following [KREY91, S. 304] for the correlation of this frequency distribution:

$$\hat{r}_{\max} = \frac{\hat{a} - (\hat{a} + \hat{d}) \cdot \hat{a}}{\sqrt{[(\hat{a} + \hat{d}) - (\hat{a} + \hat{d})^2] \cdot [\hat{a} - \hat{a}^2]}}$$
(8.14)

After insertion of the shortfall risks according to equation (8.12), one obtains:

$$\hat{r}_{\max} = \frac{\rho_C - \rho_B \cdot \rho_C}{\sqrt{\left(\rho_B - \rho_B^2\right) \cdot \left(\rho_C - \rho_C^2\right)}}$$
(8.15)

According to statistical theory, the highest value that a correlation coefficient may assume is $+1$ [BOHL92, S.235]. We intend therefore to investigate under what assumptions this value may be reached.

$$1 = \frac{\rho_C - \rho_B \cdot \rho_C}{\sqrt{\left(\rho_B - \rho_B^2\right) \cdot \left(\rho_C - \rho_C^2\right)}}$$
(8.16)

Conversion results in:

$$\left(\rho_B - \rho_B^2\right) \cdot \left(\rho_C - \rho_C^2\right) = (\rho_C - \rho_B \cdot \rho_C)^2$$
(8.17)

Multiplying out gives:

$$\rho_B \cdot \rho_C - \rho_B \cdot \rho_C^2 - \rho_C \cdot \rho_B^2 + \rho_B^2 \cdot \rho_C^2 = \rho_C^2 - 2 \cdot \rho_B \cdot \rho_C^2 + \rho_B^2 \cdot \rho_C^2$$
(8.18)

Which leads to:

$$\rho_B - \rho_B^2 - \rho_C + \rho_B \cdot \rho_C = 0 \qquad (8.19)$$

Taking out of brackets and abbreviation gives:

$$\rho_B = \rho_C \qquad (8.20)$$

$\hat{r}$ may thus only assume the value $+1$ if both individual risks are equally large. This means, on the basis of equation (8.13), that $\hat{d} = 0$. Borrower default and collateral fall short therefore always occur either simultaneously or not at all.

8.3 SHORTFALL RISK OF THE COVERED LOAN

This section is concerned with bringing together the individual elements that have been calculated to date. Equation (8.5) details the risk that both the borrower defaults and the collateral falls short, which is indeed a prerequisite for default occurring on a covered loan. This probability must be multiplied by the risk of loss $(1 - b_C)$, in order to obtain the shortfall risk of the covered loan. In proceeding thus it is implicitly assumed that only the realisation of the collateral makes breakdown distributions possible, but not the realisation of the borrower's other asset values. This does, however, make sense and is in line with the principle of conservatism.

$$(\rho_{B \cap C})^* = (\rho_{B \cap C}) \cdot (1 - b_C) \qquad (8.21)$$

By insertion of equations (8.5) and (7.41) one obtains:

$$(\rho_{B \cap C})^* = \left(\rho_B \cdot \rho_C + \hat{r} \cdot \sqrt{\left(\rho_B - \rho_B^2 \right) \cdot \left(\rho_C - \rho_C^2 \right)} \right) \cdot \frac{\rho_C^*}{\rho_C} \qquad (8.22)$$

In the special case $\hat{r} = 0$, i.e. in which there is no correlation at all, equation (8.20) reduces itself to:

$$(\rho_{B \cap C})^* = \rho_B \cdot \rho_C^* \quad \text{if } \hat{r} = 0 \qquad (8.23)$$

In the special case of the maximum correlation, equation (8.22) reduces itself, after insertion of equation (8.15) to:

$$(\rho_{B \cap C})^* = \rho_C^* \quad \text{if } \hat{r} = \hat{r}_{\text{max}} \qquad (8.24)$$

ρ_B must be determined according to the rules from Section 7.4 for applying equations (8.22) and (8.23).

In practice the challenge consists above all in determining the correlation coefficient $\hat{r}$ for the various loan transactions empirically, using statistical methods. Here one may put forward the supposition that the correlation coefficient for many loan transactions lies either close to zero (for instance, in the case of financing owner-occupied houses) or close to the maximum (for example, in the case of loans secured against collateral in the form of securities), and the application of equations (8.23) and (8.24) is therefore permissible.

In the case of a correlation close to zero it may thus well occur that the value of the collateral falls below the nominal amount of the loan, but that the borrower continues to meet his obligations. This was often the case in the financing of owner-occupied houses in the middle of the 1990s: the value of the owner-occupied house had fallen sharply in the course of the general crisis in the property market, but the borrower continued to have the same income as he had previously. It is important in such a situation that bank does not lose its nerve and call in the loan unnecessarily. It is better to profit from the low correlation by requesting moderate additional repayments (i.e. ones that are affordable by the borrower), until the value of the collateral has returned to stand at a 'reasonable' level in relation to the amount of the loan.

In the case of loans secured against collateral in the form of securities, experience is quite different. If the value of the portfolio of securities that has been mortgaged falls below the loan's nominal value, only a few borrowers are in a position to continue to service the loan out of other income. The correlation coefficient in such cases usually lies close to the maximum.

The suppositions put forward here are indeed plausible, but have yet to be corroborated empirically.

8.4 COVERED AND UNCOVERED LOANS TO THE SAME BORROWER

Both covered and uncovered loans are regularly granted to companies simultaneously. The question thus arises when assessing the individual loans of how to analyse the facts about the company. The determination of the company's shortfall risk itself is made using equation (7.48). Portraying bankruptcy proceedings in the form of a model forms another step in the assessment of the loans. Let us explain below what is meant by this.

First of all, the simplest case is assumed, in which a company's debt consists merely of one covered and one uncovered loan. It is simpler here to assess the covered loan. Because it has preferential status when it comes to bankruptcy, equation (8.22) may be applied directly.

In assessing the uncovered loan the procedure has to be analogous to that described in Section 7.9. First of all the breakdown distribution probability value has to be calculated in relation to the whole amount of loan:

$$B = \left(1 - \frac{\rho^*(L)}{\rho(L)}\right) \cdot L \cdot (1 + i_{\text{tot}}) \qquad \text{cf. (7.50)}$$

in which L corresponds here to the sum of the covered and uncovered loans.

The claim that is covered must then be deducted from this total breakdown distribution probability value. This action is consistent with the principle of conservatism. The bank that grants the uncovered loan must of course assume, in the worst-case scenario as far as it is concerned, that the preferential demand will be met in full. On the basis of the breakdown distribution probability value of the uncovered loan calculated in this way, the credit risk in relation to the loan's nominal value may be calculated according to equation (7.49).

This procedure will be illustrated by means of an example in the next section but one. We have to proceed analogously in the case of debts of complicated structures. The principle is always the same: the breakdown distribution probability values have to be determined first in total, followed by scheduling allocation of the breakdown distributions according to the Swiss laws on the recovery of debt and on bankruptcy.

8.5   RESULTS AND CONCLUSIONS

Loans where the bank relies solely on the collateral may be calculated using the same calculation rules as uncovered loans to companies. The necessary substitutions have to be made for this, as listed in Section 8.1.

Just the calculation of the volatility of securities accounts is calculated according to a slightly modified equation (8.1).

Even if a loan's collateral does fall short, this does not necessarily mean that there will be default on the loan. The borrower may nonetheless be in a position to service it. The shortfall risk is calculated in this case as follows:

$$(\rho_{B \cap C})^* = \left(\rho_B \cdot \rho_C + \hat{r} \cdot \sqrt{(\rho_B - \rho_B^2) \cdot (\rho_C - \rho_C^2)} \right) \cdot \frac{\rho_C^*}{\rho_C} \qquad (8.22)$$

As we have demonstrated, it is plausible to assume that the correlation coefficient $\hat{r}$ is very small in the case of mortgages and, in contrast, very high in the case of loans with securities as collateral. This consideration leads to the following, simpler expressions:

$$(\rho_{B \cap C})^* = \rho_B \cdot \rho_C^* \quad \text{if } \hat{r} = 0 \qquad (8.23)$$

$$(\rho_{B \cap C})^* = \rho_C^* \quad \text{if } \hat{r} = \hat{r}_{\max} \qquad (8.24)$$

Here $\hat{r}_{\max}$ is not necessarily equal to $+1$! That is only the case if $\rho_B = \rho_C$.

Combinations of covered and uncovered loans to the same borrower may be calculated. The procedure is described in the preceding section. We shall work through an example in the next section.

If, in real life, the shortfall risk of the collateral is greater than the shortfall risk of the borrower, then a partially covered loan should be calculated: the combination, therefore, of a covered and an uncovered loan.

This will be elaborated in Chapter 9, in fact in Section 9.6.

8.6   EXAMPLE

The same data is applied for this example as in subsection 7.12.1. The single difference consists in it involving a three-year fixed mortgage on a loan of three years. The allocation of breakdown distributions under the Swiss law on debt recovery and bankruptcy is:

1. mortgage
2. privileged wages and salary claims
3. uncovered loans

The correlation between the company's shortfall risk and the shortfall risk of the collateral may be set at zero.

A mortgage shortfall risk of 0.1% has been calculated according to equations (7.37)–(7.38) in Section 8.1.

The shortfall risk of the mortgage combined with the shortfall risk of the company is first calculated on the basis of this starting position. According to Table 7.6 the shortfall risk of the company over three years is $\rho_B = 11.13\%$. $\hat{r}$ continues to be equal to zero, according to equation (8.23):

$$(\rho_{B \cap C})^* = 0.1113 \cdot 0.001 = 0.011113\%$$

This corresponds to an AAA rating as per Table 2.1 with a rating risk of 0.0244%. If the risk-free rate of interest $i_s = 4.5\%$ (Table 7.5), this results — using equation (4.49) — in a mortgage rate of interest of 4.5255%, or rounded up to $4\frac{9}{16}\%$.

The assessment of the uncovered loan takes place in a second step. The probable breakdown distribution rate expected in one year comes to 93.94% according to Table 7.6. Related to the total debt of 1550 plus accumulated interest of 4.08% (Table 7.5), this yields a breakdown distribution probability value of 1515. The preferential mortgage demand, including the two years of interest to be expected of $4\frac{9}{16}\%$ of 1093, together with the privileged wages and salary claims of 62, have to be deducted from this value. This results in probable breakdown distributions of 360 for the non-preferential claims. This breakdown distribution is now allocated proportionately to the uncovered creditors of 50 and to the uncovered loan of 500 plus accumulated interest.

The value of 360 for B_C may be inserted into equations (7.61–7.65) for further calculations. This produces a corrected breakdown distribution rate of 62.74% in the case of uncovered claims of 550. (For the sake of simplicity, the creditors are also considered as claims on which interest may be claimed. This is indeed not quite correct, but the error arising is small and leads to a slightly increased risk. This is acceptable in the light of the principle of conservatism.) One then obtains a corrected loan risk of 0.2648%. This is in line with a BBB rating. The rating risk is 0.3663% according to Table 2.1. If the risk-free rate of interest i_s is 4% (Table 7.5), a loan interest rate of 4.3824%, or rounded up to $4\frac{7}{16}\%$, ensues using equation (4.49).

Comparison of the results of subsection 7.12.1 and this section (Table 8.2) gives a picture of the loan interest rate and the rating.

The company was paying annual interest of a total of 74 prior to depositing collateral, falling to 67 following doing so. The rating of the three-year loan has improved markedly, as one would expect. Conversely, however, the rating of the one-year loan has deteriorated markedly. This is on balance better both for the borrower and the bank: the borrower is paying loan interest reduced by 7 and the bank has lower loan risk on account of the collateral, which in turn takes the form of a lower total interest expectation. The lower risk for the bank ensues above all from the fact that the breakdown distribution probability values for the creditors are smaller than they were previously, following the deposit of collateral. Because of the collateral, the bank will receive a higher proportion of the breakdown distribution probability values, the

Table 8.2 Final results

Term	3-year loan without collateral		3-year loan with collateral	
1 year	AA	$4\frac{1}{8}\%$	BBB	$4\frac{7}{16}\%$
3 years	BB	$5\frac{5}{16}\%$	AAA	$4\frac{9}{16}\%$

total of which will remain the same. The depositing of collateral is, as one might expect, at the expense of the creditors.

It may be assumed, additionally, that two different banks grant the two loans. After the depositing of collateral in favour of one bank, the situation will deteriorate considerably for the other, unless it is immediately informed of the new situation and can adjust its own conditions directly to the new circumstances. The example shows clearly that in the case of borrowers that seek loans from several banks, it is absolutely essential to have, in so far as uncovered loans are granted, a restrictive clause on mortgaging in the loan agreement.

9
Calculation of the Combination of Loans with the Lowest Interest Costs

In Chapter 8 we have shown how one must proceed if a company is simultaneously seeking covered and uncovered loans. This chapter will be concerned with laying down that combination of different loans which gives rise to the lowest possible loan costs for any company.

In determining such finance for a company, the marginal interest rate of a loan is of central importance, which is why this subject is dealt with in Section 9.1 at the beginning of this chapter. Building up to the cases of two (Section 9.2) and three (Section 9.3) loans, the rules are derived for whatever number of loans one likes (Section 9.4) that lead to the financing that is the most favourable in terms of interest costs. We will demonstrate in Section 9.5 how partially covered loans may be calculated, and in Section 9.6, at what ratio of debt to equity the highest returns on equity may be achieved.

A central theme in the granting of loans is the acceptability of the debt servicing and, associated with that, the maximum degree of debt. This theme will be covered in Section 9.7 on the strength of our findings regarding the most favourable financing in terms of interest costs. The results and conclusions will be summarised in Section 9.8, and illustrated in Section 9.9 with the aid of an example.

9.1 MARGINAL INTEREST RATE

As can be seen in the figures in Section 7.5, any increase in the debt rate or mortgaging has the effect of an increase in the loan interest rate for the whole loan. The additional interest costs do, however, only arise on account of the increase itself and thus correspond in principle to the interest costs of the increase.

i_m is defined as the marginal interest rate, as the following shows:

$$i_m = \lim_{\Delta L \to 0} \frac{i(L + \Delta L) \cdot (L + \Delta L) - i(L) \cdot L}{\Delta L} \tag{9.1}$$

The marginal rate of interest thus corresponds to that rate of interest that is received, if one allocates the entirety of additional interest costs arising from an infinitesimally small increase in loan to that increase. This can be portrayed graphically as shown in Figure 9.1.

Equation (9.1) turns, as a result of multiplying out, into:

$$i_m = \lim_{\Delta L \to 0} \frac{i(L + \Delta L) \cdot L + i(L + \Delta L) \cdot \Delta L - i(L) \cdot L}{\Delta L} \tag{9.2}$$

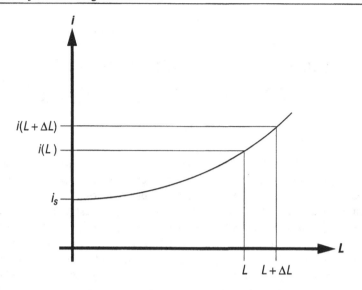

Figure 9.1

Transpositions yield:

$$i_m = \lim_{\Delta L \to 0} \frac{i(L + \Delta L) \cdot \Delta L}{\Delta L} + L \cdot \lim_{\Delta L \to 0} \frac{i(L + \Delta L) - i(L)}{\Delta L} \tag{9.3}$$

The solution of the first limit is insignificant, in that it is shortened by ΔL. In the case of the second limit, it is a question of a differential quotient. The solution, according to that, runs as follows:

$$i_m = i(L) + L \cdot \frac{\partial}{\partial L} i(L) \tag{9.4}$$

The marginal rate of interest of a loan amounting to L is thus the sum of the rate of interest of this loan together with the partial differential of the rate of interest, derived from the amount of the loan and multiplied by the amount of the loan. The problem emerges here of determining this partial differential. To anticipate the reader's question immediately — it is not possible to do so algebraically! If equation (4.49) is inserted into equation (9.4), the credit shortfall risk in equation (9.4) is preserved. As explained in Section 7.3, the credit shortfall risk has to be solved iteratively. Thus there is no other solution than to solve this differential iteratively too. There is, however, a simple possibility of determining the marginal interest rate approximately, in that in addition to the rate of interest $i(L)$, the two rates of interest $i(L + \Delta L)$ and $i(L - \Delta L)$ are calculated (see Figure 9.2).

In principle this involves determining the gradient of the interest curve at point A. As can be seen in the figure, the gradient of the straight lines through points AB is less than the gradient of the interest curve at point A. On the other hand the gradient of the straight lines through points AC is greater than the gradient of the interest curve at point A. The gradient of the

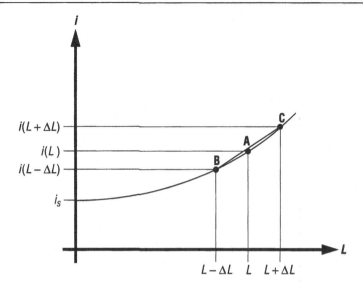

Figure 9.2

interest curve at point A thus lies between the gradients of the two straight lines described. The same applies for the gradient of the straight lines through points BC. The gradient of the straight lines though points BC may thus be selected as an approximate value for the gradient of the interest curve at point A.

The maximum absolute error that is made here corresponds to the difference in the slope of the straight lines AC and BC, which can be calculated. The value of ΔL must thus be chosen so that this difference is sufficiently small for the corresponding application of the result. The approximate value for the marginal rate of interest thus works out as:

$$i_m = i(L) + L \cdot \frac{i(L + \Delta L) - i(L - \Delta L)}{2 \cdot \Delta L} \tag{9.5}$$

Figure 9.3 shows the correlation between interest rate i and marginal interest rate i_m. It is striking that i and i_m may be approximately identical for a large field of values of d. The rise of i_m is, however, from a specified value of d onward, substantially steeper than that of i.

9.2   TWO LOANS

Every borrower's aim is to have the lowest possible interest costs. Let us assume that a borrower needs outside capital to the extent of L. This sum may be divided into two individual loans L_1 and L_2 (for example, one covered and one uncovered), such that $L = L_1 + L_2$, which means that the following applies:

$$i_1 \cdot L_1 + i_2 \cdot L_2 = \min \quad \text{with } L = L_1 + L_2 \tag{9.6}$$

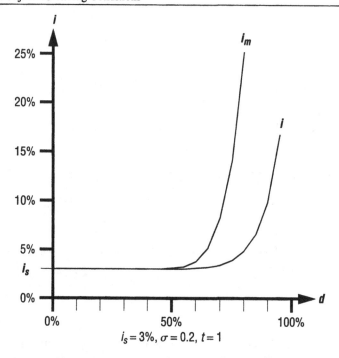

$i_s = 3\%, \sigma = 0.2, t = 1$

Figure 9.3

By expressing L_2 as $L - L_1$, the variable L_1 now has to be determined in such a way that minimum interest costs arise. L_1 has to be chosen in such a way that the first derivation from equation (9.6) at L_1 results in zero:

$$\frac{\partial}{\partial L_1}[i_1 \cdot L_1 + (L - L_1) \cdot i_2(L - L_1)] = 0 \qquad (9.7)$$

According to the rules of differential calculus, one obtains:

$$i_1(L_1) + L_1 \cdot i_1'(L_1) - i_2(L - L_1) - i_2'(L - L_1) = 0 \qquad (9.8)$$

Reverse substitution of $L_2 = L - L_1$ gives:

$$i_1(L_1) + L_1 \cdot i_1'(L_1) - i_2(L_2) - L_2 \cdot i_2'(L_2) = 0 \qquad (9.9)$$

But from equation (9.4) this is none other than:

$$i_{m1} = i_{m2} \qquad (9.10)$$

Thus the lowest interest costs arise when the overall amount of loan is so divided that the two marginal interest rates are identical. That is plausible too, as otherwise part of any loan could be replaced by making an increase in the other loan on more favourable conditions.

9.3   THREE LOANS

This is done in the same way as in the preceding section. Equation (9.8) is written here as follows:

$$i_1 \cdot L_1 + i_2 \cdot L_2 + i_3 \cdot L_3 = \min \quad \text{with } L = L_1 + L_2 + L_3 \tag{9.11}$$

Now there are two variables, L_1 and L_2. That means there are two partial differentials to be formed following L_1 and L_2, which must both be equal to zero. First the partial differential following L_1 is formed:

$$\frac{\partial}{\partial L_1}[i_1 \cdot L_1 + i_2 \cdot L_2 + (L - L_1 - L_2) \cdot i_3(L - L_1 - L_2)] = 0 \tag{9.12}$$

According to the rules of differential calculus, and following reverse substitution of $(L - L_1 - L_2) = L_3$, one obtains:

$$i_1(L_1) + L_1 \cdot i_1'(L_1) - i_3(L_3) - L_3 \cdot i_3'(L_3) = 0 \tag{9.13}$$

This again gives:

$$i_{m1} = i_{m3} \tag{9.14}$$

The partial differentiation following L_2 ensues, analogously:

$$i_{m2} = i_{m3} \tag{9.15}$$

This leads to the final result:

$$i_{m1} = i_{m2} = i_{m3} \tag{9.16}$$

In this case, too, the financing that is the most favourable in terms of costs is attained when all marginal interest rates are identical.

9.4   THE GENERAL CASE OF SEVERAL LOANS

This involves generalising the findings of the two preceding sections. We will thus investigate the situation in which a borrower seeks n loans and wishes thereby to achieve interest costs that are as low as possible. The following therefore applies:

$$\sum_{j=1}^{n} L_j \cdot i_j = \min \quad \text{with } L_n = L - \sum_{j=1}^{n-1} L_j \tag{9.17}$$

There are now $n - 1$ variables $L_1 \ldots L_{n-1}$. $N - 1$ partial differentials have therefore to be formed, and these may be written in the following way:

$$\frac{\partial}{\partial L_k} \cdot \left[L_k \cdot i_k(L_k) + \sum_{\substack{j=1 \\ j \neq k}}^{n-1} L_j \cdot i_j L_j + \left(L - L_k - \sum_{\substack{j=1 \\ j \neq k}}^{n-1} L_j \right) \cdot i_n \left(L - L_k - \sum_{\substack{j=1 \\ j \neq k}}^{n-1} L_j \right) \right] = 0 \tag{9.18}$$

According to the rules of differential calculus, one obtains:

$$i_k(L_k) + L_k \cdot i'_k(L_k) - i_n(L_n) - i'_n(L_n) = 0 \tag{9.19}$$

for all k with $1 \leq k \leq n - 1$

But this is again none other than:

$$i_{mk} = i_{mn} \quad \text{for all } k \text{ with } 1 \leq k \leq n - 1 \tag{9.20}$$

So it also applies in the general case, that a company has the most favourable outside finance in terms of interest costs when all marginal interest rates are identical.

It is worth reflecting at this point that the marginal interest rates are, at the end of the day, dependent on the term of the loan. If loans with different terms are now optimised with each other, then it must be taken into account that the optimisation may no longer necessarily be attained at the time of the next extension of a loan, as the conditions of the other loans are bound to have been firmly agreed. The optimum solution in such situations has to be found by using model calculations on the basis of various scenarios.

9.5 PARTIALLY COVERED LOANS

It is frequently the case in banking practice that loans to companies are partially covered, i.e. the value of the collateral is lower than the amount of the loan. This may make perfectly good sense in certain situations, but we will not go into the reasons here.

A partially covered loan is, in the meaning of the theory described here, none other than the combination of a covered and of an uncovered loan. First of all therefore the division between the two part loans that is the most favourable in terms of interest costs must be determined according to Section 9.2 for the calculation of this loan. Then each part loan must be assessed according to Chapters 7 and 8, and the risk-adjusted rate of interest worked out. The rate of interest for the loan as a whole is then worked out at the end as the weighted average of the rates of interest for the two part loans, on the basis of the proportion that each bears to the total loan.

9.6 MAXIMUM RETURN ON EQUITY

All entrepreneurs strive to achieve maximum return on equity invested. One means to that end is the optimisation of the ratio between debt and equity. How to do that will be demonstrated below, where it will be assumed that the long-term average return on assets is fixed. There is no inconsistency here, even if the return on overall assets is volatile in itself and in relation to itself. As better years and worse years succeed each other, a more stable average may result.

The following new variables are introduced:

return on assets: $v = EBIT/V$
return rate: $g = company\ profit/V$
return on equity: $e = company\ profit/E$

On the basis of these definitions we can write:

$$g = v - i(d) \cdot d \tag{9.21}$$

$$e = \frac{g}{1-d} = \frac{v - i(d) \cdot d}{1-d} \tag{9.22}$$

In order to attain the maximum return on equity e, the debt rate d must selected in such a way that the differential of equation (9.22) from d is equal to zero:

$$\frac{\partial}{\partial d} \left[\frac{v - i(d) \cdot d}{1-d} \right] = 0 \tag{9.23}$$

According to the rules of differential calculus, one obtains:

$$-(i'(d) \cdot d + i(d)) \cdot (1-d) + v - i(d) \cdot d = 0 \tag{9.24}$$

Solving by v one obtains:

$$v = i(d) \cdot d + (i'(d) \cdot d + i(d)) \cdot (1-d) \tag{9.25}$$

This is, however:

$$v = i(d) \cdot d + i_m(d) \cdot (1-d) \tag{9.26}$$

Equation (9.26) means precisely that any company has a debt/equity ratio that leads to a maximum return on equity, if the debt rate is selected in such a way that the interest costs, plus equity capital, multiplied by the marginal interest rate of the debt structure that has the most favourable interest costs, corresponds to its EBIT. In individual cases this condition may again only be solved iteratively.

On the basis of the derivation the above statement applies in principle only for one company with one loan. The general case with n loans can be derived likewise. The return on equity now amounts to:

$$e = \frac{v - \sum\limits_{j=1}^{n} i(d_j) \cdot d_j}{1 - \sum\limits_{j=1}^{n} d_j} \tag{9.27}$$

Whereby the debt rate was analysed into the n parts of the individual loan d_1 to d_n. Now n partial differentials have to be formed. The first runs as follows:

$$\frac{\partial}{\partial d_1} \left[\frac{v - i_1(d_1) \cdot d_1 - \sum\limits_{j=2}^{n} i_j(d_j) \cdot d_j}{1 - d_1 - \sum\limits_{j=2}^{n} d_j} \right] = 0 \tag{9.28}$$

According to the rules of differential calculus, one obtains:

$$-[i_1' d_1 \cdot d_1 + i_1(d_1)] \cdot \left(1 - d_1 - \sum_{j=2}^{n} d_j\right) + v - i_1(d_1) \cdot d_1 - \sum_{j=2}^{n} i_j(d_j) \cdot d_j = 0 \tag{9.29}$$

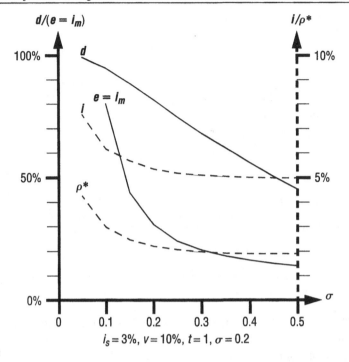

Figure 9.4

Solving by v and abbreviated with $d = d_1 + \sum\limits_{j=2}^{n} d_j$ one obtains:

$$v = i_{m1} \cdot (1 - d) + \sum_{j=1}^{n} i_j(d_j) \cdot d_j \qquad (9.30)$$

The first summand is again the equity rate multiplied by the marginal interest rate, and the second summand corresponds to the average rate of interest on debt. It was demonstrated in the preceding section (9.4) that the debt is structured at its most favourable in terms of interest costs, when marginal interest rates are identical for all loans. The marginal interest rate i_{m1} in equation (9.30) may thus be replaced by the general marginal interest rate i_m. The rate of interest that provides finance at the most favourable rate in terms of interest costs, according to the preceding section (9.4), must be inserted as the marginal rate of interest.

The maximum return on equity may thus be calculated as:

$$e = \frac{v - \sum\limits_{j=1}^{n} i_j(d_j) \cdot d_j}{1 - \sum\limits_{j=1}^{n} d_j} \qquad (9.31)$$

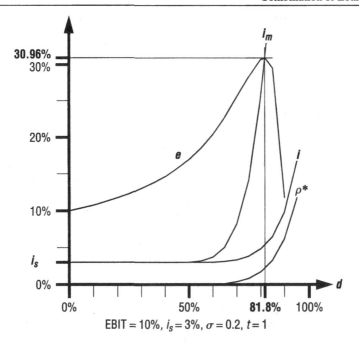

Figure 9.5

According to equation (9.30) this is:

$$e = \frac{i_m \cdot (1 - d) + \sum_{j=1}^{n} i_j(d_j) \cdot d_j - \sum_{j=1}^{n} i_j(d_j) \cdot d_j}{(1 - d)} = i_m \qquad (9.32)$$

i.e., the maximum achievable return on equity corresponds to the marginal interest rate of the debt structure that is the most favourable in terms of interest costs in the case of any appropriate ratio of debt to equity. Figures 9.4 and 9.5 elucidate this correlation for any company with one loan.

It may be recalled at this juncture that the market value, and not the balance sheet value, has been used for the value of companies in preceding chapters. The statements made in this section in relation to equity and return on equity must therefore be related to the market value:

equity = market value less debt

Maximum return on equity has therefore been derived on equity as defined above, and not on equity as defined by the company's books of account.

Figure 9.4 shows that high returns on equity may be achieved when the volatility of the value of the company is low, even if the debt rate selected is very high and even if the credit shortfall risk and loan interest rate are correspondingly high. The graphs, however, also make it clear that the most important objective for any company must be to attain the lowest possible volatility in its market value, in order to achieve the highest possible return on equity with high debt rates (cf. also comments on Figure 7.8).

Conclusions

The marginal interest rate i_m is always larger or equal to the rate of interest i. For the condition of equation (9.26) to be fulfilled, the rate of interest i must therefore be lower than the return on assets, and the marginal interest rate and return on equity respectively higher than return on assets.

High volatility in the company's market value and high rates of debt mean high interest rates, and vice versa. It follows from this that, in the case of return on assets being equal, any company the market value of which has higher volatility has a lower debt rate leading to a maximum return on equity, than a comparable company, and vice versa.

If a company is financed by loans over different terms, then the capital structure that leads to maximum return on equity should be investigated by model calculations, with the aid of different scenarios (see preceding Section 9.4). Here due heed should be given to the notion of safety.

It is discernible from the course of return on equity e in Figure 9.5 that it is dangerous to finance a company in such a way that maximum return on equity is achieved. Even small increases in the debt rate lead in this situation to sharply reduced returns on equity.

The quintessence of this section results in the following: on the assumption that all banks come to apply risk-adjusted loan conditions as described in this study, it is absolutely essential for any company to keep revenues — and thus its market value — at the highest possible level, with as little volatility as possible, in order to achieve a high return on equity via a high level of debt made possible thereby.

9.7   ACCEPTABILITY OF DEBT SERVICING

In the preceding chapters we have demonstrated how risk-adjusted loan interest rates may be calculated. What has until now been left out of consideration is whether the interest rates so calculated are in general acceptable for companies. It obviously makes no sense at all to finance any company at a high debt rate, if the risk-adjusted debt servicing that results from it leads straight to bankruptcy.

9.7.1   Acceptability of Interest Rates

In the preceding section we have demonstrated how the financing structure of a company may be determined with the maximum achievable return on equity. The most important conclusion at that point is the following: the loan interest rates of a company financed from the point of view of maximum achievable return on equity are lower than its return on assets. We must be clear here that the return on assets has been calculated on the company's market value and not on its assets as defined in its books of account. If this condition is fulfilled, the acceptability of the interest is automatic.

9.7.2   Acceptability of Repayment

When it comes to repayments, the question that arises first and foremost is why repayments should be demanded from the bank at all. It may be argued that so long as a company is paying risk-adjusted interest, it makes no sense for a bank to demand repayments — by doing so it would indeed be passing up, at least partially, good business.

The answer to this question is illustrated in Figure 9.5. In the example selected there, the company achieves a maximum return on equity if the debt rate is about 82%, and a return on equity of about 31% results from that. The interest rate on the debt amounts at this point to about 5%, according to the *i*-curve. It is evident from the course of the *e*-curve that even very small increases in the debt rate lead to a rapid falling away of return on equity, because the bank has, as a countermove, to raise the risk-adjusted loan interest rate sharply. In the case of a debt rate of 90%, the risk-adjusted loan interest rate is doubled to almost 10% and the return on equity sinks by about two-thirds to the same figure, of about 10%.

The consequence of the course of the *e*-curve is therefore that it is dangerous to finance a company to the level that matches maximum return on equity. Just one small but sharp drop in earnings and the ensuing drop in market value, and the increase in debt rate arising therefrom leads immediately to financing on the basis of sharply reduced return on equity, and may even lead to a case for winding up. In view of the danger outlined above, the optimum debt rate in the example illustrated in Figure 9.5 lies somewhere between 60% and 80%. The return on equity then is always still between 20% and 30%.

The following is now relevant as far as repayments are concerned. Let us take for granted that any good, i.e. profitable, company wishes to expand and has to invest accordingly. It may be instructed to make an increase in its debt rate, under which it might come close to the point of being financed at the level at which return on equity is maximised. In doing so it would, however, run into the dangers outlined above. It makes sense in such situations for the bank to agree on repayments that in turn lead the company away from the financial point at which such dangers arise.

So the question that comes up now is at what level repayments should be set by the bank, such that they are acceptable to the company. The upper limit here is reached if the company's owners pass up dividend payouts completely. Then all of the free cash flow remaining after interest and taxation may be applied to repayments. On the other hand this then means also that there is nothing left there at all.

The following may now be relevant, reverting to the example in Figure 9.5. Let us take for granted that the debt rate has risen to 80% as a result of new investment. The return on equity then amounts to about 30%, i.e. the profit on equity of 20% of the company's market value amounts to about 6% of the company's market value. It follows from this that the company could actually reduce the debt rate from 80% to 74% within one year. If the owners of the company are entitled to 10% dividend payout, then the repayment is reduced to 4% of the company's market value. Then debt goes down within three years, other things being equal, to below 70% and is then probably back again in the area that is safe. (To be correct, in this example taxation should also have been taken into account. This was waived for the sake of simplicity.)

9.7.3 Maximum Debt

It has become clear from the expositions made in this section so far that no company should be granted more loans than are appropriate to the financing of it for maximum return on equity. It is, however — as outlined — dangerous to approach this maximum too closely. Just how far a bank wishes to go, and with what levels of repayment — and how quickly — it wishes to lead its borrower back from this danger point is, at the end of the day, a business policy decision. The economic environment does of course play a major part in this too.

9.7.4 Consequences for Companies with Declining Earnings

Any bank in the business of lending money must be prepared for companies seeking loans having to accept sharp drops in earnings. Here we intend to examine the resulting consequences.

A sharp drop in earnings for any company that has been safely financed as described above, means — logically — that the following scenarios have occurred:

- reduction in the company's market value
- increase in debt rate
- possible increase in the volatility of the market value
- increase in the risk-adjusted loan interest rate
- the debt rate having been drawn close to that at which return on equity is maximised or having exceeded it (see Figure 9.5).

The consequences resulting for the bank are:

- increasing the loan interest rate
- demanding repayments, in order to attain the required safety distance from the maximum debt rate (see Figure 9.5).

Provided the sharp drop in earnings does not occur too suddenly — i.e. providing the necessary repayments are still acceptable to the company (see subsection 9.7.2) — there is no risk for the bank. If it is pursuing the lending policy described above logically, it is in a position to make ongoing adjustments to the debt rate that are appropriate to the situation. If the company's revenues fall so far that its market value becomes identical to its liquidation value, then the result is logically, on the basis of the expositions in this section, a maximum debt rate close to zero in relation to liquidation value. Thus the bank has no problem.

The situation is quite different if a sharp drop in earnings occurs very suddenly. The company is then no longer in a position to make the repayments that would be required to reduce the debt rate to the necessary level concerned. Thus there arises a case for the bank to wind up.

9.7.5 Consequences for Loan Supervision

Derived from the expositions in this section so far, the following tasks arise for the bank in the context of loan supervision:

- supervision of the free cash flows of the company seeking loans
- derived therefrom, supervision of the company's market value and of its volatility and of its debt rate

- regular calculation of the maximum debt rate appropriate to the maximum return on equity (see Figure 9.5)
- checking whether repayments have to be demanded in order to get back to the safety interval away from the maximum debt rate, as defined as a matter of business policy
- laying down fresh risk-adjusted loan conditions
- handing over care of the company seeking the loan to the bank's winding up department, to the extent that the company may no longer be able to make the necessary repayments, if required.

It must be any bank's objective that winding-up cases only arise, if the sharp drop in revenues that befalls the company seeking the loan comes so rapidly that the repayment requirements arising necessarily from that are no longer acceptable to the company. In all other cases the necessary repayments should be called in consistently, as explained, in order to protect the bank from damage.

9.8   RESULTS AND CONCLUSIONS

The marginal interest rate of a loan plays a central part in the calculation of the financial structures that are most favourable in terms of interest costs, and in the determination of the maximum debt rate:

$$i_m = i(L) + L \cdot \frac{\partial}{\partial L} i(L) \tag{9.4}$$

Several loans to the same company are structured most favourably in terms of interest costs if all marginal interest rates are identical:

$$i_{mk} = i_{mn} \quad \text{for all } k \text{ with } 1 \leq k \leq n - 1 \tag{9.20}$$

The maximum achievable return on equity for a company corresponds to the marginal interest rate described above, where the debt structure is appropriate.

$$e = i_m \tag{9.32}$$

Companies with a debt rate that is higher than that of the maximum return on assets are in very serious danger of going bankrupt. This therefore is also the maximum debt rate at which the bank should still be providing finance. It is, however, recommended not to go so far in the provision of outside finance that this situation is reached, in order to be able to prevent bankruptcy in the case of sharp falls in earnings occurring.

As long as a company has no more outside capital than matches the debt rate for maximum return on equity, the interest is still acceptable. The maximum acceptable repayments correspond to the return on equity after taxation. The maximum debt rate, particularly in the case of the financing of far-reaching growth, is thus also bound up with the question of whether the return on equity repayments permits the possibility of the debt rate returning 'sufficiently rapidly' to a 'bankruptcy-resistant' debt rate (see subsection 9.7.4).

In order to avoid cases of bankruptcy where there are sharp drops in earnings as outlined (Section 9.7), the bank must consistently call in the necessary repayments. If it does not do so, then bankruptcy is as good as inevitable.

9.9 EXAMPLE

The example in subsection 7.12.1 may again serve as the basis. It is intended that the loan of 1000 over three years should, however, now be guaranteed, not as in the example in Section 8.6 by a mortgage on a building, but by two mortgages on two different properties, on the most favourable conditions in terms of interest costs. The two properties have the characteristics shown in Table 9.1.

This results in the following values for the interest curve, whereby only that part of the table that is interesting for the purposes of the example is shown in Table 9.2. The credit risks ρ^* result from the application of equations (7.37)–(7.38). The risks $\rho^*_{B \cap C}$ are again the product of ρ^* times 0.1113 according to Table 7.6 as in the example in Section 8.6. The rate of interest i is calculated according to equation (4.49), whereby the risk-free rate of interest according to Table 7.6 again amounts to 4.5%. The marginal interest rate is calculated according to equation (9.5). The total interest results from the sum of the two mortgage amounts per line, times the loan interest rate concerned. (Please note: if the figures in the following table are checked, rounding differences may appear. The figures were originally calculated using an Excel worksheet to an accuracy of several more decimal points.)

The total incidence of interest is at its smallest (48.42), if House A is mortgaged at 460 and House B at 540. At these figures the difference between the two marginal interest rates is also, as one would expect, at its lowest. This now leads to the financing shown in Table 9.3.

The difference between the two rounded up rates of mortgage interest amounts to $\frac{5}{8}$%. This shows clearly that not just the rates of interest, but the marginal interest rates, must agree with each other, in order to achieve optimum financing.

Table 9.1 Starting out position

	Market value	Volatility of market value
House A	800	50%
House B	600	10%

Table 9.2 Marginal interest rates

	House A					House B				
mortgage	$\rho^*(\%)$	$\rho^*_{B \cap C}(\%)$	$i(\%)$	$i_m(\%)$	mortgage	$\rho^*(\%)$	$\rho^*_{B \cap C}(\%)$	$i(\%)$	$i_m(\%)$	Total interest
430	3.98	0.44	4.96	6.91	570	3.11	0.35	4.86	13.65	49.07
440	4.38	0.49	5.01	7.14	560	2.09	0.23	4.74	10.32	48.62
450	4.80	0.53	5.06	7.38	550	1.41	0.16	4.66	8.37	48.43
460	5.25	0.58	5.11	7.63	540	0.94	0.11	4.61	7.11	48.42
470	5.73	0.64	5.17	7.90	530	0.62	0.07	4.57	6.26	48.54
480	6.24	0.69	5.23	8.19	520	0.40	0.04	4.55	5.67	48.75
490	6.78	0.75	5.29	8.49	510	0.25	0.03	4.53	5.27	49.04

Table 9.3   Final results

	House A	House B
Mortgage	460	540
Risk ρ^*	0.58%	0.11%
Rating	BB	A
Rating risk (Table 2.1)	0.757%	0.171%
Risk-free rate of interest	4.5%	4.5%
Mortgage interest rate	5.297%	4.697%
Mortgage interest rate rounded up	5 5/16%	4 11/16%

That House B in this example — in the case of finance that is at its most favourable in terms of interest costs — is mortgaged at a much higher rate than House A, although its market value is significantly lower, is connected with the much lower volatility of the market value of House B in comparison with House A. The figures for this example were deliberately chosen to obtain results that would be as illustrative as possible.

Part IV
Implementation in Practice

Procedure — according to the model — for assessing the risk in lending to a company

Applications

Final considerations

10
Procedure — According to the Model — For Assessing the Risk in Lending to a Company

In the normal course of events representatives of the lending bank discuss their business with representatives of the loan receiving company at least once per annum, with the aid of annual and/or intermediate accounts. We will demonstrate in this chapter how to proceed in this, in order to be able to find out about the necessary model parameters as reliably as possible.

10.1 OVERALL VIEW OF THE PROCEDURE

The following values have to be ascertained using equations (7.37) and (7.38): debt rate, volatility of assets and term of loan.

The debt rate is worked out as the quotient of the outside capital divided by the value of the assets. The value of the outside capital is taken from the balance sheet. The value of the assets is determined, according to subsection 7.4.1, on the basis of the discounted future free cash flows. The free cash flows achieved in the past provide a clue for these, which must in turn support a forecast of the future asset values. The discount rate results from the CAPM. As was explained further in subsection 7.4.1, the value of the assets may never be smaller than their liquidation value. A check must therefore be made as to which of the two values is the greater (discounted free cash flows or liquidation value).

The volatility of the assets results from analysis of a range of annual accounts and budgets. It follows from this that there must be a track record in terms of annual accounts for there to be any successful loan analysis. Budgets should be brought into the calculations too, in order to take account of influences that may come to bear on volatility in the future.

The following documentation must therefore be brought together for the loan assessment:

- A complete set of the company's past accounts, it being unimportant whether they are annual, six-monthly or quarterly accounts, as long as they have been drawn up according to the same principles. An important question here is how far back into the past to delve. One answer to this question is — 'as far as possible, in order to obtain the broadest possible statistical basis'. Another answer is: 'only so far as the company's past operational situation lines up with its current operational situation, in order to avoid bringing into the assessment any factors that are now no longer relevant'. So the answer to the question of how many sets of accounts from the past should be included in the assessment is far from trivial, and does in fact have to be answered afresh on each occasion.

- Reliable budgets for the future. Here more value should be ascribed to reliability than to any far sight into the future. Clear ideas ought, however, to exist at least for the current and for the following financial year. If not, one is entitled to raise the question of whether the company's management has sufficient specialist capabilities for the company to be credit-worthy at all.
- The necessary figures, according to CAPM, for determining the discount rate: return on the market, yield of a risk-free investment in government bonds, and the extent to which the non-mortgaged assets are at risk in the marketplace.
- The remaining terms and notice periods of loans that have already been granted.

In the following sections we will on the one hand explain how this documentation should be analysed. On the other hand we will go, in each case, into what values are critical for the analysis and which must therefore be probed appropriately in discussion with the company's representatives.

10.2   ANALYSIS OF EARNINGS STATEMENTS

As mentioned in the preceding section, the determination of free cash flow is involved in the analysis of earnings statements. According to Brealey and Myers [BRMY96, S. 71/72] the following applies:

$$\text{Free cash flow} = \text{revenues} - \text{costs} - \text{investments}$$

The task is thus set, of determining sales, operating costs and investments. Here it must be ensured that the operating costs do not contain any depreciation or interest on debt, as it is the value of the company's assets that have not been mortgaged that has, according to the model, to be determined.

In portraying sales in earnings statements it is often necessary to establish that distinctions are made between operational and non-operational, and between ordinary and extraordinary revenues. Such distinctions are of no importance at this point. Once the company's management has decided that the enterprise should embark on certain activities, these then become an element in the company's activity and therefore form part of its risk profile. So all the company's revenues must be added together when it comes to determining revenue.

The same applies for costs as explained above in respect of revenues. All costs with the exception of depreciation, provisions and interest on outside capital must be taken into account.

Other figures in earnings statements are irrelevant in connection with analysing loan risks. In particular depreciation and provisions are of no interest in this context, as they do not feature in the calculation of free cash flow.

When discussing accounts it should be ensured that the complete sales and operating costs for all existing accounts and budgets can be found out as precisely as possible. Net positions should be subdivided again into their individual elements, as the result is otherwise distorted.

10.3   ANALYSIS OF CASH FLOW STATEMENTS

The amount of investments is still missing for determining free cash flow. This is worked out from the cash flow statement, and here all investments must be taken into consideration in turn.

And here too, as already explained in the preceding section, no possible distinctions should be preferred according to the various categories.

When discussing accounts it should therefore be ensured that the company's previous and planned investment activity can be found about comprehensively. All the figures necessary for calculating the free cash flows are thus determined.

10.4 ANALYSIS OF BALANCE SHEETS

Under the model, the value of a company's assets are worked out either from the value of the discounted free cash flows or from the liquidation value of the assets, whichever value is the larger. It follows from this that in respect of the assets only their possible liquidation value in the event of bankruptcy should be determined. Or, put another way — neither the current operational value of the assets, nor the company's depreciation and provision policy, are of any significance for the analysis of credit risk.

On the liabilities side of the balance sheet it is only the current and planned debts budgeted *vis-à-vis* third parties that are of interest, in order to be able to determine the current and future debt rate. Here any possible categories of loans must be taken into account. In order to evaluate privileged claims correctly, subordinated debts such as equity must therefore be considered. It follows from this that the calculation of the debt rate must be undertaken separately for each loan, if need be according to which category it falls into. Here only debts in the category having precedence or in the same category have to be taken into account.

When discussing accounts it should therefore be ensured that the liquidation value of the assets can be found out about as precisely as possible. If the debts are proved, it may be assumed that these are correctly stated. If they are not, then it could be a case of falsification of documents.

10.5 DETERMINATION OF THE DISCOUNT RATE

In order to determine the respective value of assets, the discount rate applicable at that moment must be determined for each set of accounts, for the discounting of the free cash flows. How the CAPM may be used for determining the discount rate was explained in summary in subsection 7.4.1. The determination of the risk measurement β plays a decisive role here. The relevant β can be calculated as follows in the case of companies quoted on the stock exchanges [BRMY96, S. 215]:

$$\beta_V = \frac{D}{V} \cdot \beta_D + \frac{E}{V} \cdot \beta_E \tag{10.1}$$

β_V = risk measurement of the value of the company
β_D = risk measurement of the debts
β_E = risk measurement of the equity

It may be assumed here that the values for β_E and β_D are available from suppliers of information such as Bloomberg or Reuters. Should a company have only quoted shares and not bond loans as well, then the value for β_D should be supported by values of companies in the same or related sectors.

The determination of β is more difficult in the case of companies that are not quoted. One solution here is to use the calculation of the β-values of quoted companies in the same or related sectors, as described above. Such comparisons are admittedly not simple in Switzerland, as only a few companies are quoted compared with larger countries. Foreign values can possibly be used by way of comparison too. This question too may only be answered, at the end of the day, by empirical testing. The higher β-values should be used in comparisons, under the principle of conservatism. Otherwise we refer, at this juncture, to appropriate reading (for example [BRMY96, Chapter 9: Capital Budgeting and Risk]).

10.6   DETERMINATION OF RELEVANT LOAN TERMS

When determining the relevant term for the loan using the model, the question comes up of how long will it be until the bank granting the loan gets its money back.

The relevant loan terms result primarily from the loan agreements. In the case of fixed-rate loans, it is a question of the residual term until maturity. In the case of all other loans, the notice period is definitive. Here it must, however, be ensured that critical situations are normally recognised only following a periodic discussion of accounts. Moreover, the duration of the proceedings in any possible bankruptcy must be taken into account. So the following terms ensue, which must be inserted into the model:

- In the case of fixed-rate loans, the term relevant to the credit risk corresponds to the residual term plus the possible duration of any bankruptcy proceedings.
- In the case of loans on which notice can be given and of no fixed duration, the term relevant to the credit risk corresponds to the sum of the time until the next discussion of accounts, plus the notice period, plus the possible duration of any bankruptcy proceedings.

It follows from this that the volatility that is dependent on the term of the loan, and thus the credit risk, may be lowered to the extent that the terms of fixed-interest loans, the periods of notice, or the intervals between discussions on accounts are kept short.

10.7   DETERMINATION OF VOLATILITY

The volatility of the company's value may be calculated, according to subsection 7.4.2, on the basis of the values calculated — per set of accounts and per budget — for the free cash flows, for the discount rates and for the liquidation values.

10.8   DETERMINATION OF CREDIT RISK

As soon as all values have been calculated as described in the preceding sections, the shortfall risk of each of the company's loans can be determined as described in Section 7.3.

The method will be illustrated in Chapter 11, with the aid of three examples.

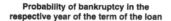

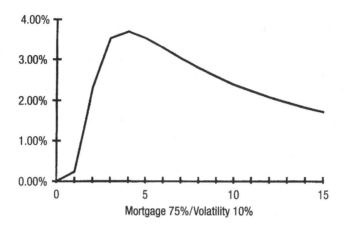

Figure 10.1

10.9   PRUDENCE IN THE CASE OF NEW LOANS/BORROWERS

It has been possible to observe, empirically, that default on loans occurs much more frequently at the beginning of the term than after a certain duration (see, for example, [FRRM97, S. 112]). That is to say loans which can already point to some duration are much safer for the bank granting them than newly approved loans.

This fact can be understood from the model described here. (The values for the mortgage and volatility were selected for Figure 10.1 in such a way that the resulting curve is about the same as in [FRRM97, S. 112].)

It is therefore advisable to have particular caution prevail in the case of new business transactions, such that figures based on pessimistic expectations are inserted into the model. It is furthermore recommended that new loans are checked more frequently at the beginning of their terms.

The recognised rating agencies behave in just this way when it comes to assessment of asset-backed and mortgage-backed securities. It is an advantage for a bank to put together for securitisation portfolios of loans in which the loans already have higher seasoning. In these cases the rating agencies demand smaller loan reinforcements for the achievement of a top rating than for portfolios with newly granted loans.

10.10   POSSIBLE CAUSES OF CONFLICT BETWEEN BANK AND BORROWER WHEN THE MODEL IS APPLIED

The application of the model described demands a fair amount of specialised knowledge and experience, not only from the bank personnel concerned. Demands are made on borrowers, too, in that they are tending to have to furnish more, and more detailed information about their companies. This requires appropriate knowledge, on top of willingness to share. Such operational knowledge may, however, not be presupposed to exist in all small and medium-sized enterprises. It follows from this that auditors commissioned to produce annual accounts have to receive broadened mandates, which entails matching extra costs.

As was explained in Section 9.6 and illustrated in Figure 9.5, the response on the bank's part to any company having a high debt rate must be the application of appropriately higher loan interest rates. If the rules described in Chapter 9 are kept to, these interest rates are also acceptable to the borrower and still make operational sense because it may increase its return on equity without running irresponsible risks. Such high-risk premiums on loan interest rates — as calculated by the model in some circumstances — have, however, been unusual in Swiss banking practice hitherto. Readiness to pay such interest rates if appropriate still has to be stimulated. This will be all the more difficult, and take all the longer, while other banks (still) do not apply loan conditions that are consistent with risk.

Particularly for the two reasons outlined above, application of the model may lead to conflict between bank and borrowers:

- The scope of the information required will be seen as an unreasonable demand.
- The additional costs for auditors will be viewed as pointless expenditure.
- The high loan interest rates will seem to threaten commercial viability, even if that is not the case.

These causes of conflict should be countered by careful training of the bank officials concerned and where applicable the borrowers, by means of detailed explanations. It does of course go without saying that this is far from simple. The application of risk-adjusted loan conditions, combined with the careful examination of credit-worthiness required for that, is, however, imperative for the continued existence of any bank. The commercial difficulties experienced by some banks at the beginning of the 1990s, not least owing to far-reaching financing of property and the excessively low mortgage interest rates that were associated with it, and to insufficiently careful checks on credit-worthiness, have clearly proved this [BRUN94, S.137 and thereafter].

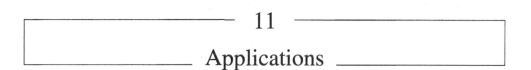

11

Applications

In this chapter, first of all, we will investigate three practical cases and compare the results with the conventional assessment made by the lending bank concerned. All figures we have given are not the actual sums in Swiss francs that were concerned, thus making it impossible to draw conclusions about the identity of the bank customers involved and maintaining bank confidentiality. The proportions that the figures in any example bear to each other do, however, match, in order to make for accurate analysis. Only in Section 11.3 may checking come up with some minor discrepancies, as the change in the starting values led to smaller changes in the proportions, while the results were calculated using the original figures.

11.1 SPECIALIST CLOTHING BUSINESS: TURN-AROUND SITUATION

This example is about an established business specialising in ladies' and gentlemen's clothing, with shops throughout Switzerland, in a turn-around situation. Annual accounts for the last five years, and budgets for the current year and for the next two years ahead, were available for analysis. Those in the bank responsible for the customer considered the company's budgets very reliable, on the strength of their previous experience, so these were used for the analysis.

First the EBIT for the individual years is calculated and then capitalised using the long-term market return of 7%, whereby it is assumed implicitly that a value of $\beta = 1$ is, according to the CAPM, applicable in this case. Then the company's liquidation value for the individual years is determined from its assets, using normal banking correction factors. The higher of earning capacity value and liquidation value is taken as the market value for further calculations. The applicable debt rate is calculated with reference to outside capital owed to third parties. An approximate figure of 20% of annual wages and salary costs is inserted for privileged salary claims in the event of bankruptcy, so that the corrected loan risks are calculated (see Section 7.9): the figures below are obtained, if one inserts 4% for the standard rate of interest. Volatility is worked out using equation (7.45) on the basis of the company's market value. Loans are in each case granted for one year. The Excel worksheet in Appendix 2 is used for the calculations, and the results are summarised in Table 11.1.

In recent years this customer was classified by the bank as an increased credit risk, which is fully understandable on the basis of the above analysis. A new management team, assessed as competent, took over responsibility for the company at the beginning of the 1990s, and in 1995 an external 'turn-around' adviser was brought in as well. The loan was therefore continued, in the hope of better times.

The budgets for 1999 to 2001 are encouraging, and on the strength of their past reliability, the turn-around expected for 1999 seems actually to be in sight. So those responsible for the client

Table 11.1 Specialist clothing business: model information and results

	Five annual accounts					Three budgets		
Year	94	95	96	97	98	99	00	01
EBIT	70	84	66	76	74	100	106	122
Earning rate	1000	1200	943	1086	1057	1429	1514	1743
Breakup value	1060	960	920	800	820	820	820	800
Market value	1060	1200	943	1086	1057	1429	1514	1743
Debts				1076	1048	1000	972	908
Debt rate (in %)				99.1	99.1	70.0	64.2	52.1
Privileged salaries				56	58	60	60	60
Volatility of the market value:		calculated:	17.7%					
		rounded:	20.0%*					
Annual credit shortfall risk (in %)			24.5	24.3	0.37	0.12	0.004	
Corrected annual credit shortfall risk (in %)			49.0	49.6	0.66	0.22	0.009	
Rating according to Table 2.1			DD	DD	BB	BBB	AAA	

* Volatility was rounded up to 20% to take uncertainties into account.
NB: The figures for 1994 to 1996 were not calculated out, being of no further interest by spring 1999.

have applied to the loan assessment office for the client to be assigned to a higher category of credit-worthiness within the bank. As this application is only supported by budgets, it seems premature. Before anything is undertaken on this, the positive prospects should at least be confirmed by means of a set of intermediate accounts as at 30.6.99. Such intermediate accounts have been being obtained for a long time, anyway, because of the strained credit-worthiness situation.

This example allows us to show, impressively, that loan risk assessment must be underpinned by parameters set in the future because — on the basis of the current situation — the loans to this company would have had to be terminated without notice. The positive prospects for the future do, however, allow their continuation to appear appropriate. When it comes to setting the interest rate here, this may neither be based on the current situation (too pessimistic) nor on the budget projection (currently as yet too optimistic). This combination of circumstances calls, rather, for the interest rate to be set on the basis of what the company can accept to pay.

An EBIT for 1999 of 100 is budgeted for distribution. Equity as per the balance sheet of 31.12.98 comes to 82. The earnings reported for 1999 should therefore be split into 100 parts, of which 5 remain as earnings and 95 are set aside for debt servicing. The bank-related debt amounts to 938, the remaining debt being non-interest-bearing positions such as creditors. An average rate of interest on debt of 10% is realistic for the bank in the context of the budget being attained. But in order not to jeopardise the turn-around by imposing excessively high interest costs, at least a part of the loans might be converted into a profit participating loan with returns thereon being dependent on success.

The conventional loan decision and the loan decision emerging from the use of the model are qualitatively identical in this example. The advantage of the model consists, however, in the fact that the risks involved are quantifiable and appropriate loan supervision measures may be laid down. The uncertainties regarding the quality of budgeting, the development of the market and of the sector, and the capabilities of the management team were taken into account with an increase in volatility. Here it is once again shown that establishing the figure for volatility is of decisive importance. The banker's experience plays an important part in this.

11.2 COMPANY TRADING IN MACHINE TOOLS: PROVISION FOR SUCCESSOR COMPANY

The two major shareholders in a company trading in machine tools each own 48.5% of its share capital. They form the management team, together with a third person who owns the remaining 3% of the shares. The older of the two major shareholders would like to withdraw from the business, and offers the younger his shares at a price of 240. The latter intends to form a holding company to acquire the shares. He applies to the bank seeking a loan for the full purchase price, whereby he would pledge the entire shareholding of 97% in his ownership in favour of the loan. He intends, on the basis of a freshly drawn up business plan, to repay the loan over five years, with payments of 48 per annum.

Only the 97% of the future dividends of the trading company will be available to service the debt. Disregarding minor management costs, this dividend income corresponds to the company's EBIT. The loan application has therefore to be examined on this basis. The three most recent sets of annual accounts and five forward budgets of the trading company are available for this examination. EBIT will again be capitalised at 7% in order to determine the company's market value. The liquidation value of the company matches the current value of the shares. Analysis of the figures made available has resulted in the company's market value in all years having been higher than its liquidation values.

The relevant figures are shown in Table 11.2 (calculations with the help of the worksheet in Appendix 2).

An average loan risk of 5.1% results, based on the 1997 annual accounts. With a standard rate of interest of 4%, this makes a loan interest of about 10%. This leads in 1998 to a debt

Table 11.2 Trading company: model information and results

Year	3 Annual accounts			Five budgets				
	95	96	97	98	99	00	01	02
*Holding-EBIT	15	13	52	93	97	98	101	98
*Market value	214	186	743	1329	1386	1400	1443	1400
Market value volatility			56.8%					
rounded			60.0%					
loan			240	240	192	144	96	48
**Duration loan			3.0	3.0	2.5	2.0	1.5	1.0
Credit shortfall risk (t) (in %)			14.7	5.1	1.64	0.28	0.007	0.0
Average annual credit shortfall risk (in %)			5.1	1.7	0.66	0.14	0.005	0.0
Rating according to Table 2.1			CC	CCC	BB	A	AAA	AAA

* Corresponding to 97% of the dividends of the trading company.
** Disregarding interest.
NB: The figures for 1995 and 1996 were not calculated out, being of no further interest by spring 1998.

service of 24 (interest) + 48 (repayment) = 72. This is acceptable under the 1998 budget, but not in relation to the 1997 accounts. Any reduction in the repayment would, conversely, lead to an extension in the duration and thus increase the loan risk and interest rate. That is therefore no solution. The budgets do, moreover, seem really rather optimistic, viewed in relation to the past. The loan application should therefore be declined on the grounds of questionable acceptability.

It is apparent from this example that budgets that are very optimistic compared with past performances do lead to high volatility in a company's market value. In this case, considerable loan risk would have ensued from minor mortgaging of just about one-third (240/743 = 0.329). Related to any operating company, this means that any fast growth must be financed above all by its own cash flow, because of the high volatility associated with it: finance using bank loans becomes rapidly associated with high risks that lead, in turn, to matching high (too high!) interest costs.

For this loan application the bank had also established by conventional methods that it should refrain from granting the loan. The business was not done. The questionable acceptability was also decisive. The budgets were assessed as being too optimistic when it was taken into account that an experienced member of the management team was leaving the company.

The qualitative loan decision reached both by conventional means and via the model was identical in this example too. The model does, however, deliver detailed reasoning for having to turn down the loan application.

11.3   SHIP MORTGAGES: RISK LIMITATION

This example is all about figuring out where the risk in the loan transaction lies.

11.3.1   Starting Position

A major shipowner has had a group of six bulk tankers financed by a consortium of eight banks. Ship mortgages have been set up for this purpose. The ships were built in 1976/77. As a result of costly special surveys the value of the ships, according to estimates by two internationally respected firms of shipbrokers, was put at a total of 1000 at 29.9.98. The scrap metal value of the ships at the same point in time amounted to 212. The loans were 378 at 30.6.98.

The shipowner applied in the middle of 1998 to increase the loans to 450, in order on the one hand to finance refitting costs and on the other to have liquid funds available for the purchase of new ships. The banks granted the loan application on the strength of the low proportion of the ships' value mortgaged and of the fact that it had been possible to extend their working lives through to the middle of 2003, thanks to the refits. Cash flow analysis of future revenues worked out that ships' incomes of about 0.11 per day at sea would suffice to cover the costs of operating and maintaining them, and the loan costs.

11.3.2   The Banks' Loan Decision

The banks consented to the increase in the loans and agreed with the shipowner the repayment plan in Table 11.3. Due note was taken that the loan outstanding of 171 as at 30.0.03 would

Table 11.3 Ship mortgages: model information

From end of quarter	Amortisation	Loan	Depreciation	Ship value	Debt rate (in %)	High volatility (in %)	Low volatility (in %)
III 98		450		1000	45.0	43.0	27.0
IV 98	13.1	436.9	41.5	958.5	45.6	41.8	26.2
I 99	15.2	421.7	41.5	917.0	46.0	40.6	25.4
II 99	19.8	401.9	41.5	875.5	45.9	39.4	24.6
III 99	13.6	388.6	41.5	834.0	46.6	38.2	23.8
IV 99	13.6	374.7	41.5	792.5	47.3	36.9	23.1
I 00	13.6	361.1	41.5	751.0	48.1	35.7	22.3
II 00	18.0	343.1	41.5	709.5	48.4	34.5	21.5
III 00	13.6	329.5	41.5	668.0	49.3	33.3	20.7
IV 00	13.6	315.9	41.5	626.5	50.4	32.1	19.9
I 01	13.6	302.3	41.5	585.0	51.7	60.9	19.1
II 01	18.0	284.3	41.5	543.5	52.3	29.7	18.3
III 01	13.6	270.7	41.5	502.0	53.9	28.5	17.5
IV 01	13.6	257.1	41.5	460.5	55.8	27.3	16.7
I 02	13.6	243.5	41.5	419.0	58.1	26.1	15.9
II 02	18.1	225.4	41.5	377.5	59.7	24.8	15.2
III 02	13.6	211.8	41.5	336.0	63.0	23.6	14.4
IV 02	13.6	198.2	41.5	294.5	67.3	22.4	13.6
I 03	13.6	184.6	41.5	253.0	73.0	21.2	12.8
II 03	13.5	171	41.0	212	80.7	20.0	12.0

certainly have been covered by the scrap metal value of the ships. The positive decision was above all underpinned by the following considerations:

- At 45%, the proportion of value mortgaged was small at the time of the increase in the loans.
- The loan repayment at the end of the ships' lives — the 'balloon' payment — is well covered by the scrap metal value of the ships that was expected at that time.
- According to the bank's calculations the break-even freight rate amounts to about 0.09 per day, based on details supplied by the shipowner and on comparison with similar ships — the current freight rate of 0.11 per day was thus quite well sufficient.
- The ship owner's management team was judged to be very capable and reliable.

11.3.3 Assessment of the Loan Risk by the Banks

The bank that made the documentation available had assessed the loans with a loan risk of 80 basic points according to its internal rating system. This classification was made on the strength of comparisons with loans in similar positions.

11.3.4 Determination of Loan Risk According to the Model

Additional factors for determining loan risks according to the model must include the volatility of ship prices and of scrap metal prices, realisation costs in the event of bankruptcy, time scales and ship depreciation:

Volatility

Details from the spring 98 issue of the bi-annual *Clarkson Shipping Review and Outlook* — from the Clarkson firm of shipbrokers — were used for determining the volatility. Both the time series from 1979 to 1998 for the tankers in question (Page 16, column 280k 1975) and the relevant scrap metal prices (Page 153) are to be found there. The following volatility figures for each of the years concerned may be calculated by using this information:

Ship prices:	1979–98:	43%
	1993–98:	27%
Scrap-metal prices:	1979–99:	20%
	1993–98:	12%

Behind the use of two different time periods is the consideration that the 1979–98 sequence of numbers allows calculation of the worst case, and the five-year 1993–98 period is most likely to be representative for the last part of the term of the loans. As it was possible to depreciate the ships using the straight-line method (see below), it may be assumed for the sake of simplicity that volatility of the ship prices moves in line with volatility of the scrap-metal prices (see Table 11.3).

Realisation Costs in the Event of Bankruptcy

These amount to about 4.5 per ship, according to the bank's information. Costs of about 27 have therefore to be allowed for six ships.

Time-scale Considerations

The loan agreement contains a clause covering the event of default. Thus, if the shipowner is at any point not in a position to service the debt on time, then the consortium of banks has the right to make the loan repayable immediately and to realise the value of the ships. According to the bank's information, such ships can be realised within three to six months, be it privately or by means of auction. The loan may be utilised on a roll-over basis in the form of advances in Euro of, in each case, terms of from one to 12 months. The longer-term advances have intermediate interest deadlines, in each case after three months. So every three months the banks may establish whether the shipowner is still in a position to service its debts. On top of the time needed for realisation of the ships, a reaction time of from six to nine months is worked out for the banks. The following risks are examined in terms of their time-scale aspects on the basis of this situation:

- High volatility: 6, 9, 12 and 15 months from the most recent proper payment service the debt.
- Low volatility: 6, 9, 12 and 15 months from the most recent proper payment service the debt.

Depreciation of the Ships

According to the bank's information, the ships may be depreciated using the straight-line method from their current value of 1000 as at 29.9.98 to their scrap value of 212 as at 30.6.03.

Table 11.4   Ship mortgages: results in %

Whole term	Low volatility 0.5070%				High volatility 2.8073%			
	Term				Term			
From end of quarter	6 months	9 months	12 months	15 months	6 months	9 months	12 months	15 months
III 98	0.0004	0.0077	0.0318	0.0749	0.2025	0.6320	1.1287	1.6099
IV 98	0.0003	0.0063	0.0271	0.0653	0.1795	0.5751	1.0398	1.4939
I 99	0.0002	0.0048	0.0219	0.0545	0.1530	0.5091	0.9373	1.3610
II 99	0.0001	0.0030	0.0151	0.0401	0.1156	0.4142	0.7904	1.1724
III 99	0.0001	0.0024	0.0127	0.0346	0.1022	0.3762	0.7273	1.0868
IV 99	0.0001	0.0021	0.0113	0.0314	0.0886	0.3369	0.6613	0.9968
I 00	0.0001	0.0017	0.0097	0.0276	0.0797	0.3101	0.6148	0.9320
II 00	0.0000	0.0011	0.0069	0.0207	0.0617	0.2569	0.5265	0.8135
III 00	0.0000	0.0009	0.0060	0.0185	0.0568	0.2404	0.4961	0.7692
IV 00	0.0000	0.0008	0.0054	0.0169	0.0537	0.2294	0.4746	0.4368
I 01	0.0000	0.0008	0.0051	0.0161	0.0527	0.2245	0.4634	0.7179
II 01	0.0000	0.0005	0.0038	0.0124	0.0427	0.1927	0.4085	0.6423
III 01	0.0000	0.0005	0.0039	0.0129	0.0460	0.2013	0.4200	0.6357
IV 01	0.0000	0.0007	0.0046	0.0146	0.0537	0.2230	0.4525	0.6921
I 02	0.0000	0.0010	0.0062	0.0184	0.0699	0.2669	0.5158	0.7719
II 02	0.0000	0.0011	0.0069	0.0202	0.0716	0.2705	0.5216	0.7721
III 02	0.0001	0.0028	0.0137	0.0353	0.1266	0.4027	0.7119	0.9997
IV 02	0.0007	0.0102	0.0373	0.0802	0.2839	0.7136	1.1211	1.4655
I 03	0.0095	0.0607	0.1487	0.2512	0.8509	1.5808	2.1343	2.5463

The model information needed according to the above expositions may be taken from Table 11.3. The results are summarised in Table 11.4. It was assumed, in the case of the calculations of the quarterly loan risks, that the situation as it was then is presented as in Table 11.3, and that the shipowner had up until then met its commitments fully on each occasion. The calculations were made with the aid of the worksheet in Appendix 2.

As may be seen in Table 11.4, the loan risk is heavily dependent on the bank's reaction time. The figures in the case of 15 months are significantly higher than for six months, under the assumption both of the lower and of the higher rates of volatility. It becomes apparent that assessment of the volatility of the value of the collateral and the bank's reaction time acquire decisive significance in the case of this loan.

It is more difficult to frame the risk calculation over the full term. The assumption was first of all made that servicing the debt had until then taken place in full at the beginning of any calendar quarter. It had therefore been worked out at first, for calculating the loan risk, how big it would have been on the assumption that the remaining debt was still outstanding at that point in time. Then the same loan risk was calculated as at the end of the quarter, and the loan risk was determined for that quarter from the two figures taken together. The weighted average, in terms of amount, of these risks per quarter, converted to one year, then give the loan risk per annum over the entire term (Table 11.4).

A situation assessment has to be carried out first of all, because of the high influence of the bank's reaction time on the loan risk in the event of default. The amount of the loan, the current value of the ships and the volatility of the development in value may not be influenced. On the other hand, realisation of the ships may or may not be forced in terms of time, depending on the risk situation. So it has to be assessed whether it is more advisable for the bank to realise a lower price in the short term, or whether it should attempt to achieve, over a somewhat longer time-scale, a price that is higher but still uncertain.

11.3.5 Comparison of Assessment between the Bank and the Model

There is a credit shortfall risk of about 51 basic points on the assumption of the lower rate of volatility, considered over the full term of the loan. But as every three months it can be viewed again whether the shipowner is or is not still meeting its commitments, this is a worst-case scenario. Seen from the point in time at which the loan is discussed there results, for each individual quarter for three or six months (i.e. including the time expected for realisation) a normal credit shortfall risk of less than one basic point. Only for the last two quarters are the figures correspondingly higher, because of the higher proportion of mortgage existing at that point, but they are still very small. It follows that the bank assessment is too pessimistic on the assumption of the lower rate of volatility.

For reasons of conservatism it may be argued that a credit rating must be aligned to a longer than normal realisation period. As may be gathered from Table 11.4, however, loan risks that are still less than five basic points result from reaction times of 12 and 15 months (corresponding to realisation periods of 9 and 12 months), except in the last two quarters.

There is a credit shortfall risk of about 2.8% on the assumption of the higher rate of volatility, considered over the whole term of the loan. It is only here that the decisive influence of the volatility figures used becomes apparent. But this too is again a worst-case scenario. From the point of view of the individual quarters, and with the exception of the last quarter, figures of from 4 to 72 basic points emerge for the two shorter reaction times. In the final quarter the figures are again somewhat higher. It follows from this that the bank assessment lines up more or less with the figures for the higher rate of volatility taken from the model. Only in the case of reaction times of one year or more would the risk have to be estimated as being higher.

It follows from the above reflections that the bank assessed this loan very cautiously. When considered in this sort of way, the bank's assessment is more or less in accordance with the model's results for higher volatility rates. If volatility is, however, justifiably estimated less pessimistically, then the bank — without further ado — may classify the loan one level better, in line with its internal rating system, i.e. with 25 basic points credit risk. (The bank later decided on the more optimistic evaluation of the position.)

11.3.6 Limitation of Loan Risk

The results in Table 11.4 show that the credit risk rises sharply if the time taken to realise the ships were to draw further out or if the credit risk is considered over the entire term of the loan. The more optimistic evaluation of the credit-worthiness of this ship mortgage can thus only be justified if:

- The credit-worthiness can be reassessed every three months, and if necessary the default clause can be invoked.
- The short time-scale for realising the ships, of from three to six months, is considered to be realistic.
- The volatility rate for the value of the ships is assessed, on the basis of a five-year time-scale – in line with the residual term of the loan — on the optimistic side.
- The shipowner's management team is considered capable of operating the ships over the coming five years in line with revenue expectations.

The above listing of preconditions, and of the relevant influencing factors involved, does on the one hand show where the credit risks can be limited. It does, however, also become clear that a bank requires much experience in the field of financing international shipping to be able to operate this sort of business profitably.

This example shows plainly that, thanks to the model, the credit risk may both be quantified and also limited. It may also be demonstrated what risks the bank runs if the necessary loan supervision measures are not undertaken. The model's informative value is therefore substantially higher than conventional methods of loan assessment.

11.4   MORTGAGE BUSINESS 1985–99

Over the period 1990–95 the banks in Switzerland were confronted with high losses on mortgage business. Our intention now is to examine whether this situation could have been foreseen with the aid of the model. The property index drawn up by the Cantonal Bank of Zürich provides the basis for the calculations (see Appendix 3).

Figure 11.1 gives a graphical representation of the course of the index. It makes it clear that the index is at its most volatile for multiple dwelling units. The mortgage business is

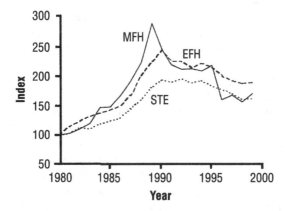

MFH is the abbreviation of the German text for multiple dwelling unit.
EFH is the abbreviation of the German text for single-family home.
STE is the abbreviation of the German text for condominium.

Figure 11.1

Table 11.5   Volatility of the index in % — for multiple dwelling units as per Appendix 3

Year	4 Index values	5 Index values	6 Index values	Maximum
1985	10.8	8.6	7.9	10.8
1986	10.7	8.5	7.4	10.7
1987	7.7	8.5	7.4	8.5
1988	1.5	6.7	7.4	7.4
1989	7.6	6.8	9.3	9.3
1990	24.2	19.2	16.4	24.2
1991	25.7	21.7	19.1	25.7
1992	6.9	20.2	18.7	2.2
1993	6.7	7.9	17.2	17.2
1994	2.2	5.5	7.3	7.3
1995	3.6	3.8	6.2	6.2
1996	21.3	17.6	15.0	21.3
1997	23.2	18.4	15.9	23.2
1998	20.5	18.2	15.6	20.5
1999	9.4	19.4	17.2	19.4

therefore investigated, using this index, in what follows. The course of the volatility is detailed in Table 11.5. This was calculated for each calendar year with the help of the figures for the last four, five and six year's indices, such that three, four and five quotients respectively were available for the calculation (see equation (7.45)).

The highest volatility figure concerned is given in each line in the last column of Table 11.5. These figures are used later in the course of this analysis to define a worst-case scenario. This means that both the influences both of short- and long-term volatility are included in the later calculations. It is of course debatable whether this is the right way to proceed. For the purposes of this example, however, the volatility in each case per annum is determined in this way. The figures in the table are shown graphically in Figure 11.2. It is striking that the volatility figures show a clear peak at the beginning and at the end of the 1990s. The cause is in the first place the sharp increase in the index figures and the subsequent sudden transition to a decline in prices, and the uneven development in the second half of the 1990s.

Two assumptions *vis-à-vis* mortgages are made for the credit shortfall risk calculation. The first assumption is that a multiple dwelling unit in 1985, i.e. well before the mortgage loan crises at the beginning of the 1990s, is mortgaged at 80% of its saleable value. The amount of the loan is left unchanged in subsequent years, without repayments, which leads to different mortgage figures in each year corresponding to the course of the index. The credit shortfall risk figures calculated in this way demonstrate how they developed for the bank over the years, in line with the assumption that neither repayments of them, nor increases in them, took place.

The second assumption is that in each calendar year in each case a multiple dwelling unit is mortgaged again to the extent of 80% of its saleable value. The credit shortfall risk figures calculated in this way demonstrate what sort of risk the bank was running in each calendar year concerned by financing to the extent of 80%.

Table 11.6   Credit shortfall risk development in % under the assumptions

Year	1985	1986	1987	1988	1989	1990	1991	1992
Ann. 1	0.09	0.00	0.00	0.00	0.00	0.01	0.10	0.02
Ann. 2	0.09	0.08	0.01	0.00	0.03	3.27	3.91	1.82
Year	1993	1994	1995	1996	1997	1998	1999	2000
Ann. 1	0.00	0.00	0.00	0.99	0.88	1.07	0.28	
Ann. 2	0.98	0.00	0.00	2.18	2.85	1.90	1.57	

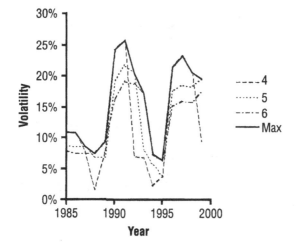

Figure 11.2

As may be inferred from Table 11.6, the credit shortfall risks under the first assumption were very small even during the crisis at the beginning of the 1990s. Under the second assumption, however, they became plainly higher than previously at the beginning of the 1990s. As early as 1990 the figure was so high that 80% mortgages in that year were no longer appropriate. This situation repeated itself towards the end of the 1990s. The facts are portrayed graphically in Figure 11.3. Annual volatility figures were used for the calculation. Appropriately higher figures should be used when granting fixed mortgages over several years, which leads to credit shortfall risks that are correspondingly even higher.

It becomes clear from Table 11.6 and Figure 11.3 that the mortgage loan crisis, based on the annual index figures, was foreseeable from the model as early as the beginning of 1991, after the index figure for 1990 came into existence. By using quarterly figures it may be assumed that the reaction time could have been reduced even further.

It would be interesting, in the immediate future, to track down whether the credit shortfall risks rates that have just risen again are leading to a second mortgage loan crisis in the near

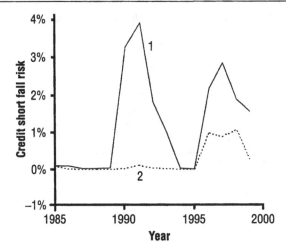

Figure 11.3

future, or whether the necessary safety precautions, on the basis of the experiences banks have had, have been taken.

On the strength of this result the usefulness of the model proves itself, at least in qualitative terms. Whether or not the results are also sufficiently accurate in quantitative terms could only be established by comprehensive empirical testing. Such testing would, however, far exceed the scope of this study.

12

Final Considerations

So far we have emphasised that the method of calculating risk-adjusted loan interest rate presented here is only a theory. Theories have to be examined empirically in order for their validity to be corroborated (see Section 1.8). It was also pointed out that this empirical testing would exceed the scope of these expositions. We will nonetheless outline in Section 12.1 how this testing should be undertaken.

We will explain in Section 12.2 how a bank wishing to introduce the method described here must proceed, and in Section 12.3 what the preconditions are for its applicability. We will at the same time point out how closely the empirical testing, introduction and applicability are connected with each other.

In Section 12.4 possible customer considerations will be discussed, and in Section 12.5 the questions still open will be summarised. We will conclude this study with some closing remarks in Section 12.6.

12.1 TESTS OF HYPOTHESES

The method presented here is a theoretical, mathematical model for calculating the risks involved for banks in their lending business. As the examples in the separate chapters show, the results of the method are plausible as they match up in qualitative terms with the experience of banks in this business. That does not, however, yet necessarily mean that the results are also precise in quantitative terms. So it is necessary, in the next step, to test the method empirically (see Section 1.8 too).

The construction of the empirical test is once again based on the concept of insurance. So it has to be tested empirically, whether the *ex ante* forecasts losses agree with the *ex post* actually established losses using the method presented here. But this is none other than the comparison of imputed 'insurance premiums' with actual 'loss experience' (cf. Section 1.8; [BCBS99, S. 50:a] backtesting). It follows from this that the empirical examination must be built up by analogy with preliminary and actual costing in the insurance industry. And here checks must be undertaken, using recognised statistical tests (cf. for example [BOHL92]) to determine whether deviations between forecast and actual losses are coincidental, or whether they follow a pattern.

Deviations that are coincidental lead to the conclusion that the theory does hold up. Deviations that follow a pattern may have two causes:

• that the theory does not hold up;
• that the parameters selected do not hold up.

It is above all the determination of the 'correct' rates of volatility that is difficult, as may be inferred from subsection 7.4.2 and from the reading referred to there. In the cases of deviations that follow a pattern it must therefore, above all, be checked whether any better agreement between the forecast and the actual losses might have been achieved by selection of 'better' volatility rates. Then we must find out how such 'better' volatility figures could have been determined *ex ante*. Only if this approach is unsuccessful should the theory be rejected (cf. Section 1.8 [BCBS99, S. 50: b) and c)]).

An independent examination of the method of procedure is also needed so that the model, if required, becomes acceptable for regulatory purposes (cf. Section 1.8 [BCBS99, S. 50: d)]).

The expenditure required for the empirical testing outlined should not be underestimated in any way at all. This becomes evident as one becomes aware of the prerequisites, which can be subdivided into three main groups:

- Creating the preconditions for the application of the method described here.
- Creating the preconditions in operational accounting terms (also, possibly, with customers).
- Creating the preconditions for the facts to be analysed.

Preconditions for the Application of the Method Described Here

These will be elaborated in the next section.

Preconditions in Operational Accounting Terms

In order to obtain the widest possible factual basis for statistical tests which in turn allows for the most varied analyses, it is necessary from the start to record the following facts for each loan utilised:

- The agreed risk insurance premium $r \cdot L$ (see equation (1.1) for each interest period. Depending on whether or not the method is already being applied in the test phase on a 1/1 basis, either the risk premiums actually demanded of the customer are determined, or the risk premiums calculated according to the model on the basis of the theory are obtained and imputed.
- The precautionary provisions actually made for each interest period, divided — for the purpose of further analyses — into those required for regulatory purposes and those required operationally for the banks' own estimating purposes.
- The losses actually incurred in each interest period.
- The figures necessary for determining correlations in each interest period (see subsection 12.2.2 on 'statistical bases', subheading 'correlations').
- The operational expenditure (personnel costs, etc.) incurred in processing winding up operations in each interest period. These costs do not in fact have anything directly to do with the costs of risk discussed here, but they have to be covered too and, indeed, by profit contributions $p \cdot L$ (cf. Section 1.5, equation (1.1)). Even today there is probably not even one bank that is aware of how high are the costs of processing just one single case of winding up. If the operational accounting is already in place, then this too may be foreseen at the same time.

Clearly the expenditure required on IT for this is considerable, but it is nonetheless essential for achieving our purposes. Simplifications may be made, if need be, at a later stage, if the theory has proved well founded and when it has been possible to gather together the first experiences of its application by converting unique data into composite data, up to a certain point.

It is necessary to get right on top of the data flow that the facts described above will form. For this, in turn, the necessary IT resources have to be made available. On top of that banks will have to recruit the necessary specialist staff who must be capable of designing and evaluating statistical tests. Leading bank officials, actuaries and economists familiar with the methods described here will have to work together in such specialist teams. It must be assumed that focused management of such a heterogeneous team will be critical.

The action described above will clearly be very expensive in time and money. The implementation of empirical testing must therefore be carefully planned, and budgeted for, in the form of a project. The costs that are budgeted and the ongoing costs that will then arise have to be set against the losses on loans that have been incurred in the past, and which have exceeded the dimensions they were expected to have at the time. It is at this juncture that we venture to forecast that this comparison will indeed demonstrate that the expenditure for such a project will be justified.

12.2   IMPLEMENTATION IN PRACTICE

We can group the preconditions that must be fulfilled for the putting this method into practice, as follows:

- specialist personnel
- statistical bases
- IT support
- organisational measures

12.2.1   Specialist Personnel

The necessary specialist personnel must be recruited for successful implementation of this method, both in the offices that assess and wind up loans.

Loan Assessment Offices

The will must be there to recruit specialist personnel who have sufficient financial and mathematical knowledge to be able to understand this theory. As becomes evident from the illustrations in Section 7.5, the granting of loans for large ranges of mortgage and volatility ratings is completely without problems. It is also the case that a majority of bank loans consists of standard transactions such as advances against securities, financing of owner-occupied houses, and financing of small companies on current account credit. It may be assumed that the great majority of such business can be processed by standard, IT-supported procedures.

But specialists who are capable of making their own calculations are needed for assessing more demanding loan transactions — whether it is more complex loan structures that are concerned, or financing arrangements that are more far-reaching. The results in these cases in particular must be probed, and subjected to sensitivity analysis, for inaccuracies. A more profound understanding of this theory is needed for such cases, even if much can be made easier by IT support.

Winding Up Offices

The specialists in winding up offices must be capable, above all, of undertaking the calculations described in Section 9.6. Some of this can most probably be standardised in terms of IT, in cases of loan transactions with simple structures.

Sales

Sales staff must be capable of explaining the loan conditions that have been calculated to customers. They must most of all be able to demonstrate, using illustrations, the correlations between mortgage, volatility and loan interest. These play an especially important part in advances against securities and the financing of owner-occupied houses. The borrower against securities is particularly concerned to prevent excess collateral for his loan being taken, while the owner-occupier is particularly interested in obtaining the highest possible mortgage on his house — especially when he is first buying it. Here it must be demonstrated, with the aid of tables and charts, that the level of mortgage in connection with volatility does have a direct influence on the loan interest level. There is thus no sense in which there can be excess collateral in the case of an advance against securities, i.e. the higher the collateral, the lower the rate of interest, and vice versa. By way of contrast, there are quite clear upper limits when it comes to the mortgaging of owner-occupied houses, where in the case of high mortgages interest rates rise sharply such that, beyond a certain point, their acceptability is no longer to be assumed. Similar considerations apply to the financing of enterprises.

12.2.2 Statistical Bases

We have referred repeatedly to the importance of having available the necessary statistical bases. The figures for volatility (see subsection 7.4.2) are particularly critical in this respect.

Financing Companies

In subsection 7.4.2 we made the assumption that, for determining the volatility of the market value of a company, some three to four sets of annual accounts and one or two budgets for the financial years ahead must be available. Two questions arise here: on the one hand it must be checked empirically, in accordance with the expositions in subsection 7.4.2, whether or not the volatility was ascertained in this way with sufficient precision. On the other hand, borrowers must be in a position to deliver all this information. Regretfully must we record, at this point, that these preconditions are not sufficiently fulfilled in the case of small and medium-sized companies. One way of improving this situation lies in the opportunity it provides for calculating volatility rates on the basis of worst-case scenarios. The resulting high loan interest might possibly motivate borrowers in future to prepare the necessary facts and figures, in order to reduce their loan costs.

Mortgages

Reliable sequences of figures on the way prices have developed in the property market are essential for being able to calculate mortgages reliably. The Cantonal Bank of Zürich has adopted a pioneering role here, in that it has demonstrated that this is possible [ZK96], with the result that today it regularly publishes a property market index for the Canton of Zürich (see Appendix 3). Work in this field must be carried further and extended to cover the whole of Switzerland.

Loans Against Portfolios of Securities

The volatility of any portfolio of securities can be determined by reference to stock exchange statistics. Here, too, empirical tests as described in Section 1.1 must demonstrate how sufficient reliability may be attained.

Correlations

The correlation between the probabilities of borrowers defaulting and of collateral falling short was studied in Sections 8.2 and 8.3. Figure 8.1 illustrated that there must be differentiation between four cases of the probabilities $\hat{a}$, $\hat{b}$, $\hat{c}$, and $\hat{d}$ occurring for the determination of the correlation. These figures must be regularly ascertained for every borrower of a covered loan, in order to be able to calculate, based on that, the correlations that will be of interest.

12.2.3   IT Support

We have already mentioned, in Section 12.1, IT support for creating preconditions in terms of operational accounting and in terms of statistical evaluation of facts. On top of that, the IT-supported method described here must be implemented by means of expert systems. Due attention must be paid to the numerical methods used, because of the complexity of the formulae, and especially of the iterative calculations. Development of such expert systems should therefore be left to software specialists in possession of estensive knowledge of numerical systems. These would normally be software developers working on technical/scientific applications. No great volumes of facts actually have to be processed in the calculations relating to any one single loan.

12.2.4   Organisational Measures

Putting this theory into practice calls for a comprehensive project, to be undertaken by staff of appropriate calibre specially trained for it. This staff has to deal with the task areas, outlined above, of staff recruitment and training, statistical bases and IT solutions.

Once the project work is concluded, a permanent specialist staff of mathematicians and statisticians must be set up, as companies in the insurance industry already know all too well. The tasks for this staff include development of the theory, handling complex special cases, keeping the statistical bases permanently up to date, and ongoing development of the IT-based aids.

12.3   APPLICABILITY OF THE METHOD PRESENTED

To be able to apply the method presented, the following preconditions must be fulfilled:

- The theory must be corroborated empirically, as described in Section 12.1.
- The operational preconditions as described in Section 12.2 must be fulfilled.

The crux of the matter here is the following: the theory must already be introduced *de facto* in order for it to be possible to test it empirically. This was indeed pointed out in Section 12.1. Here it is not so important, from the point of view of expenditure, whether the introduction is at first made partly by imputation, or wholly in transactions with customers. If a bank does decide to undertake empirical testing, then it must in actual fact be taking a *de facto* decision to bring the method in.

One way of reducing costs could lie in restricting implementation to just one part of the bank's operations (for example to one type of loan transaction, or within one limited geographical area).

That way costs, particularly for specialist staff and if need be for the working up of statistical bases, could be limited. The costs of IT and of the project team would, however, remain more or less unchanged.

The question then arises: how big is the danger of failure and what does it cost? The results of the theory are plausible in qualitative terms, as has already been mentioned at the beginning of Section 12.1. Many other examples that are not set down here have confirmed this impression. So it is permissible at this juncture to assume that absolute failure is ruled out. So the risk is rather that the method may not deliver as much as it seems to promise. This, however, is not least a question of expectations. It remains therefore a matter of weighing costs against benefits. We make no secret of the fact that banks will have to reckon with considerable costs. On the other hand, however, the possible benefits of really getting the costs of credit risks under control, are likewise considerable.

Implementation of this method would presumably be at its most simple for a bank entering into the business of lending for the first time. As such a bank would have to be building up the necessary IT structures from scratch, anyway, it might do so as suggested here. In order to limit the risk of mistakes arising from the theory, applications for loans should still be examined in the conventional manner and then checked by the method presented here. Loans should then only be granted if both methods of operation come to a positive result, and on the basis that it should be the higher rate of loan interest that is applied to the commercial transaction with the customer. This does not jeopardise the empirical test in any way at all: under the theory put forward here, interest rates that are higher than the minimum rates are certainly permissible (cf. Section 4.6). But in these cases the distinction must be drawn in operational accounting between risk premiums necessary according to the model and risk premiums that are in practice charged and collected.

This section concludes with a strong warning against making empirical testing — out of cost considerations — no more than a 'trawl' through the archives. Our own experiences with such exercises show that (a) they do not as a rule come up with the desired results, and (b) they do not really save any money.

One must not underestimate, either, the time it takes for reliable facts to accumulate. The Basel Committee itself reckoned on several years (cf. Section 1.8: [BCBS99, S. 2]). According to the terms of the loan products to be examined, it is assumed here that between about five and 10 years must be allowed. But it should also be taken into account that know-how will be building up continually — from ongoing evaluations — until the situation we are aiming for is reached.

12.4   CUSTOMER CONSIDERATIONS

As already mentioned in Section 10.10, something is both demanded and expected of the borrower when this model is applied. It should not therefore be ruled out that a bank customer might not be prepared to make the efforts demanded of it. As we explained in Section 1.3, the borrower decides, in the same way as the concept of insurance is applied, whether or not it is prepared to pay the risk-adjusted price being asked. It will not necessarily do this if more favourable counter offers are available. The bank has to make the borrower aware, in such situations, why it has reached the conclusions it has reached. The bank has to decide, on the strength of an assessment of the position — in which the overall current and future business potential of this customer and the credit risks involved with it are weighed against each other — whether or not it is willing to persevere with its offer and its demands for information. If it is sure that it has calculated the loan interest rate correctly, it will do this in its own interest, as in the last analysis it jeopardises its own existence if it makes too many concessions in respect of its price and demands for information.

It is at this point that we venture to forecast that the banks that will be successful in the long term, in the business of lending, will be those which can indeed say no — when their clients obtain more favourable counter offers from other banks — provided that they themselves are in a position to calculate risk-adjusted loan conditions correctly. From this it will follow that the borrower will have to reflect whether it always wants to go for the cheapest offer — with the disadvantage that this may be associated with frequent changes of bank partners — or whether it is on occasion prepared, in the interest of a longer-term confidence-building business relationship, to meet the bank's information requirements and to pay the price the bank has asked.

12.5   OPEN QUESTIONS

As we mentioned in Section 1.2, the subject of this study was deliberately limited. In particular we did not cover the following in terms of separate business transactions:

- borrowers in the public sector and/or ratings related to countries
- loans in foreign currencies
- international lending business, especially the financing of projects.

Furthermore the subject of portfolios of loans was likewise not covered. Efforts are being made to develop methods that scale down the shortfall risk of a whole portfolio of loans *vis-à-vis* the sum of the individual loan risks (cf. for example, [MANZ98] and the reading suggested there). To what extent the method we have introduced here may contribute anything in this field must be the subject of future studies.

12.6   CLOSING REMARKS

Some idea of the consequences of the method we have introduced here may have been communicated with the help of illustrations and examples, but it has been necessary to confine ourselves to a small selection. The meaningful content of this theory has thus not yet been fully developed by any means, and the field for further studies is therefore still wide open.

In portraying the method we have introduced, it has only been possible to give an overall view. Many details still await clarification.

So it is as true as ever that providing the answers to old questions all too often forms the starting point for posing new ones!

Appendix 1: Notation

		Equation number
$\hat{a}$	probability	8.2
b	breakdown distribution rate probability	2.4
$\hat{b}$	probability	8.2
b_c	corrected breakdown distribution rate probability	7.56
$\hat{c}$	probability	8.2
d	debt rate	7.30
$\hat{d}$	probability	8.2
e	return on equity	9.22
f	financing cost rate	1.1
g	return rate	9.21
i	loan interest rate	1.1
$i(t)$	loan interest rate according to the whole term	7.50
$i_c(t)$	corrected loan interest rate according to the whole term	7.56
i_d	discount rate	7.41
i_g	return on a risk-free investment in government bonds	7.43
i_m	marginal interest rate	9.1
i_{mt}	return on the market	7.43
i_{pa}	interest rate on annual basis	7.40
i_s	risk-free standard interest rate	1.2
i_{spa}	annual standard interest rate	7.40
p	profit contribution rate	1.1
r	shortfall risk hedging rate	1.1
r_c	correction factor	4.21
r_{cac}	current account credit write-off risk hedging rate	4.20 ·
$\hat{r}$	correlation coefficient	8.3
t	term	7.37
v	return on assets	9.21
A	number of trading days per year	8.1
B	breakdown distribution probability value	2.4

B_c	corrected breakdown distribution	7.54
C	free cash flow	7.41
C_j	cash flow face value after j periods	1.2
D	debts	7.2
E	equity	7.1
L	payed out loan amount	1.2
L_g	granted loan	4.19
L_u	used loan	4.20
N	standard normal distribution function	7.28
P	put value	7.4
R_b	billed return	4.20
R_n	necessary return	4.19
S	proportional salaries	7.54
V	value of the company	7.1
V_I	liquidation value	7.46
X	portfolio values	8.1
β	measurement of unlevered assets market risk according to CAPM	7.43
χ	survival chance	2.2
χ^*	survival chance regarding the breakdown distribution probability value rate	2.8
ε	cumulative success chance	3.2
φ	cumulative shortfall risk	3.2
x	credit-worthiness key figure	2.10
μ	medium of the logarithms	7.45
ρ	shortfall risk	2.1
ρ^*	credit shortfall risk	2.7
ρ_a	average of all n shortfall risks ρ_k	5.8
ρ_c	corrected credit risk	7.57
$\rho_{B \cap C}$	combined risk	8.2
σ	volatility of the company value according to the time period	7.28
ψ_j	probability of cash flow C_j	1.2
Γ	gamma function	7.45
Λ	loan market value	4.1

Appendix 2: Excel Worksheet

An Excel Worksheet set up as follows proved to be the best way of calculating the equations in Chapter 7. [For this iterations absolutely must be allowed under **Extras/ Options/Calculations**.]

	A	B
1	Debts L_{tot}	(Input field)
2	Amount of loan L	(Input field)
3	Term t in years	(Input field)
4	Standard interest rate i_s	(Input field)
5	Market value of the company V	(Input field)
6	Volatility of the market value σ	(Input field)
7	Privileged salary/wage claims S	(Input field)
8	Mortgage d	= B1/B5
9	Volatility according to term t	= B6*SQRT(B3)
10	x	= LN(B8/(1-B13))/B9+B9/2
11	$N(x - \sigma(t))$	= STANDNORMDIST(B10-B9)
12	$N(x)$: probability of bankruptcy ρ	= STANDNORMDIST(B10)
13	Loan risk ρ^*	= (B11-B8*B12)/(B11-B8)
14	Loan risk per annum ρ_{pa}	1-(1-B13)^(1/B3)

(*Continued*)

15	Loan interest rate i_{pa}	(B4+B11)/(1-B14)
16	Breakdown distribution rate b	1-B13/B12
17	Loan demand at maturity	B2*(1+B15)^B3
18	Breakdown distribution probability value B	B16*B17
19	Proportional privileged salary/wages claims S	B7*B2/B1
20	Corrected value of B: B_c	IF(B18>B19;B18-B19;0)
21	Corrected breakdown distribution rate probability b_c	B20* (1-B12)/(B2*(1+B4)^B3-B20*B12)
22	Corrected loan risk ρ_c^*	B12*(1-B21)
23	Corrected loan risk per annum ρ_{cpa}^*	1-(1-B22^(1/B3)
24	Corrected loan interest rate i_{cpa}	(B4+B23)/(1-B23)
25	Corrected loan interest rate on account of S	B24-B15

Hint 1:   The loan interest rates in B15 and B24 are calculated on the basis of the loan risks calculated in B14 and B23, and not on the basis of the shortfall risk of the rating level concerned according to Table 2.1. Table 2.1 may indeed be programmed in Excel, but this is very laborious.

Hint 2:   On occasion Excel manifests difficulties with this worksheet and reacts with various fault reports in the B column. If this happens click on Field B13, and then F2, and then press ENTER.

Hint 3:   In the case of unreliable figures for d (Field B7): i.e. $d \leq 0$ or $d \geq 1$; Excel runs through the maximum number of iterations (presetting usually 100; can be seen under EXTRAS/OPTIONS/CALCULATIONS) and then aborts with fault reports. Reducing the maximum number of iterations under the presetting is therefore recommended. Usually 10 will suffice.

Hint 4:   If only the loan amount in line 2 is changed from one calculation to the next, then only the values in lines 21 to 25 change in the results.

Appendix 3: Property Price Index

The Cantonal Bank of Zürich's property price index for the Canton of Zürich, dated 5 May 2000.

Year	Single-family home	Multiple dwelling unit	Condominium
1980	100.0	100.0	100.0
1981	115.0	102.9	103.1
1982	124.1	110.4	113.5
1983	132.0	120.3	110.6
1984	138.0	147.1	119.5
1985	143.5	148.8	124.6
1986	150.7	167.6	129.1
1987	167.0	192.2	144.9
1988	200.5	222.3	161.0
1989	223.2	287.5	179.6
1990	243.6	245.7	193.6
1991	225.8	219.5	189.7
1992	226.0	211.8	196.2
1993	214.6	212.6	188.9
1994	221.9	208.9	193.1
1995	216.3	218.7	183.9
1996	200.2	160.6	178.3
1997	192.9	168.4	171.4
1998	188.0	156.9	161.8
1999	190.2	171.6	162.7

http://www.zkb.ch/bin/entry/frame/private/immobilien/index.html
Source: Cantonal Bank of Zürich

Appendix 4: Chapter 3 — Derivations

First of all we calculate the values of φ_j and ε_j for each individual period of the n periods. The solution for the first period is evident:

$$\varphi_1 = \rho_1 \tag{3.3}$$

$$\varepsilon_1 = \chi_1 \tag{3.4}$$

It is assumed, for further considerations, that ρ_{j+1} and χ_{j+1} are independent of ρ_j and χ_j. For a borrower definitely either to default or not to default in the second year, it may not default in the first year. According to the laws of multiplication of probability calculus [BOHL92, S. 324] the following applies:

$$\varphi_2 = \chi_1 \cdot \rho_2 \tag{3.5}$$

$$\varepsilon_2 = \chi_1 \cdot \chi_2 \tag{3.6}$$

The same applies, by analogy, for the following periods:

$$\varphi_{j,j\neq1} = \left(\prod_{k=1}^{j-1} \chi_k\right) \cdot \rho_j = \left(\prod_{k=1}^{j-1}(1-\rho_k)\right) \cdot \rho_j \tag{3.7}$$

$$\varepsilon_j = \prod_{k=1}^{j} \chi_k \tag{3.8}$$

On the assumption that ρ_j and χ_j have the same value, in each case, for all n periods, equations (3.7) and (3.8) may be simplified as follows:

$$\varphi_j = \chi^{(j-1)} \cdot \rho = (1-\rho)^{(j-1)} \cdot \rho \quad \text{if } \rho_1 = \cdots = \rho_n = \rho \tag{3.9}$$

$$\varepsilon_j = \chi^j \qquad\qquad\qquad\qquad \text{if } \chi_j = \cdots = \chi_n = \chi \tag{3.10}$$

Under the definition above $\varphi(n)$ means the probability that the borrower will default not in any specified but in any one of the n periods. As the default may only occur in one and not in several periods, if it occurs at all, the following self-excluding events generally [BOHL92, S.

313] apply according to the laws of addition of probability calculus:

$$\varphi(n) = \sum_{j=1}^{j} \varphi_j = \rho_1 + \sum_{j=2}^{n} \left[\prod_{k=1}^{j-1} (1 - \rho_k) \right] \cdot \rho_j \tag{3.11}$$

and, especially:

$$\varphi(n) = \sum_{j=1}^{n} (1 - \rho)^{(j-1)} \cdot \rho \quad \text{if } \rho_1 = \cdots = \rho_n = \rho \tag{3.12}$$

According to equation (3.12) $\varphi(n)$ is a geometric series with $a_1 = \rho$ as its first term and the multiplication factor $q = (1 - \rho)$, under which the following applies:

$$\varphi(n) = \rho \cdot \frac{1 - (1 - \rho)^n}{1 - (1 - \rho)} = 1 - (1 - \rho)^n = 1 - \chi^n \tag{3.13}$$

The law of addition does not apply to $\varepsilon(n)$, as in contrast to shortfall, success only occurs if each individual period of the n periods was successful. $\varepsilon(n)$ thus corresponds to ε_n (cf. equations (3.8) and (3.10)). So in general the following applies:

$$\varepsilon(n) = \prod_{j=1}^{n} \chi_j \tag{3.14}$$

and, especially:

$$\varepsilon(n) = \chi^n = (1 - \rho)^n \quad \text{if } \chi_1 = \cdots = \chi_n = \chi \tag{3.15}$$

The following thus applies in the special case:

$$\varphi(n) + \varepsilon(n) = (1 - \chi^n) + \chi^n = 1 \tag{3.16}$$

which equation (3.2) confirms. In the general case the following results:

$$\varphi(n) = 1 - \prod_{j=1}^{n} \chi_j = 1 - \prod_{j=1}^{n} (1 - \rho_j) \tag{3.17}$$

Reflection now leads to the probability ψ_j, that ψ_j is none other than the probability that no loss arises within the first j periods. So in general the following applies:

$$\psi_j = \varepsilon_j = \prod_{k=1}^{j} \chi_k = \prod_{k=1}^{j} (1 - \rho_k) \tag{3.18}$$

and, especially:

$$\psi_j = \chi^j = (1 - \rho)^j \quad \text{if } \chi_1 = \cdots = \chi_n = \chi \tag{3.19}$$

Appendix 5: Chapter 4 — Derivations

SECTION 4.1 DERIVATION

According to the assumptions that were made (cf. Section 1.7), the same risk-free rate of interest for discounting is used for each summand. Furthermore, $\Lambda = L$ applies. Reducing with L and putting i outside the brackets in the first summand results in:

$$1 = i \cdot \left(\sum_{j=1}^{n} \frac{\chi^j}{(1+i_s)^j} \right) + \frac{\chi^n}{(1+i_s)^n} + \left(\sum_{j=1}^{n} \frac{\chi^{j-1} \cdot \rho \cdot b \cdot 1 + i}{1+i_s^j} \right) \tag{4.2}$$

In the case of the first summand, we are concerned with a geometric series with:

$$a_1 = \rho = \frac{\chi}{(1+i_s)} \tag{4.3}$$

In the case of the second summand, we are likewise concerned with a geometric series with:

$$a_1 = \frac{\rho \cdot b \cdot (1+i)}{(1+i_s)} \qquad \rho = \frac{\chi}{(1+i_s)} \tag{4.4}$$

So ρ is identical in both geometric series and only a_1 is different.

By using the overall equation for geometric series and substitution by equation (4.3), equation (4.2) is rewritten as follows:

$$1 = \frac{i \cdot \rho \cdot (1 - \rho^n)}{(1 - \rho)} + \rho^n + \frac{\rho \cdot b \cdot (1+i) \cdot (1 - \rho^n)}{(1+i_s) \cdot (1 - \rho)} \tag{4.5}$$

Taking the mean summand ρ^n on the left-hand side and extending by $(1 - \rho)$ results in:

$$(1 - \rho) \cdot (1 - \rho^n) = i \cdot \rho \cdot (1 - \rho^n) + \frac{\rho \cdot b \cdot (1+i)}{(1+i_s)} \cdot (1 - \rho^n) \tag{4.6}$$

The fact that the equation may be shortened at this point by $(1 - \rho^n)$, is important. This now results in:

$$(1 - \rho) = i \cdot \rho + \frac{\rho \cdot b \cdot (1+i)}{(1+i_s)} \tag{4.7}$$

So the path of the term with the time element of the number of periods n has been shortened as a consequence of the assumption that shortfall risks are constant. The key result for the shortfall risk hedging rate r comes thus to be independent of the term of the loan! Tasking i out of brackets results in:

$$(1 - \rho) = i \cdot \left(\rho + \frac{\rho \cdot b}{(1 + i_s)}\right) + \frac{\rho \cdot b}{(1 + i_s)} \qquad (4.8)$$

Reverse substitution of ρ and replacement of i by $(i_s + r)$ according to equations (1.1) and (1.3) results in:

$$1 - \frac{\chi}{(1 + i_s)} = (i_s + r) \cdot \left(\frac{\chi + \rho \cdot b}{1 + i_s}\right) + \frac{\rho \cdot b}{(1 + i_s)} \qquad (4.9)$$

Multiplication by $(i_s + r)$ and replacing χ by $(1 - \rho)$ results in:

$$i_s + \rho = (i_s + r) \cdot (1 - \rho + \rho \cdot b) + \rho \cdot b \qquad (4.10)$$

Multiplying out and insertion of $(1 - \rho + \rho \cdot b) = (1 - \rho^*)$ (see equation (2.6)) results in:

$$i_s + \rho = i_s \cdot (1 - \rho^*) + r \cdot (1 - \rho^*) + \rho \cdot b \qquad (4.11)$$

Solution by r results in:

$$r = \frac{i_s + \rho - i_s \cdot (1 - \rho^*) - (\rho \cdot b)}{(1 - \rho^*)} \qquad (4.12)$$

$$r = \frac{i_s + \rho^* - i_s + i_s \cdot \rho^*}{(1 - \rho^*)} \qquad (4.13)$$

$$r = \frac{\rho^*}{1 - \rho^*} \cdot (1 + i_s) \qquad (4.14)$$

As r is independent of n, the same shortfall risk hedging rate r must also be valid for a limitless number of periods of loan term, in which the expectation value of the repayment of capital according to Section 3.3.1 is precisely zero! This can be verified, in that equation (4.5) is written for a limitless geometric series with a limitless number of periods, thus:

$$1 = i \cdot \frac{\rho}{1 - \rho} + \rho^\infty + \frac{\rho \cdot b(1 + i)}{(1 + i_s) \cdot (1 - \rho)} \qquad (4.15)$$

As $\chi \leq 1$ always applies, $\rho < 1$ always applies on the assumption that $i_s > 0$ always applies likewise. This assumption is permissible, as there is in practice no such thing as 'free credit'. This means that ρ^∞ is a null consequence and equation (4.15) turns into:

$$1 = i \cdot \frac{\rho}{1 - \rho} + \frac{\rho \cdot b(1 + i)}{(1 + i) \cdot (1 - \rho)} \qquad (4.16)$$

$$(1 - \rho) = i \cdot \rho + \frac{\rho \cdot b \cdot (1 + i)}{(1 + i_s)} \qquad (4.17)$$

The comparison shows that equations (4.7) and (4.17) are identical and thus must lead to the same conclusion. The value

$$\rho^* = \rho(1-b) \tag{4.18}$$

is none other than the credit shortfall risk, which is dependent on the shortfall risk ρ of the borrower and on the probable breakdown distribution rate b.

SECTION 4.5 DERIVATION

The deviation ΔL from the nominal amount is calculated as the difference of:

$$\Delta L = \Lambda - L \tag{4.30}$$

This means:

$$\Delta L > 0 \text{ appreciation profit}$$
$$\Delta L < 0 \text{ need for provision to be made}$$

From (4.29) and (4.30) there results:

$$\Delta L = \Lambda - L = \left(\sum_{j=1}^{l} \frac{\chi_l^j \cdot i \cdot L}{(1+i_{sl})^j} \right) + \frac{\chi_l^l \cdot L}{(1+i_{sl})^l} + \left(\sum_{j=1}^{l} \frac{\chi_l^{j-1} \cdot \rho \cdot b \cdot L \cdot (1+i)}{(1+i_{sl})^j} \right) - L \tag{4.31}$$

Abbreviation using L results in:

$$\frac{\Delta L}{L} = \lambda = \left(\sum_{j=1}^{l} \frac{\chi_l^j \cdot i}{(1+i_{sl})^j} \right) + \frac{\chi_l^l}{(1+i_{sl})^l} + \left(\sum_{j=1}^{l} \frac{\chi_l^{j-1} \cdot \rho_l \cdot b \cdot (1+i)}{(1+i_{sl})^j} \right) - 1 \tag{4.32}$$

In the case of both summands, we are again concerned with geometric series. By using the appropriate overall equations, there results:

$$\lambda = \frac{i \cdot \frac{\chi_l}{(1+i_{sl})} \cdot \left(1 - \frac{\chi_l^l}{(1+i_{sl})^l}\right)}{\left(1 - \frac{\chi_l}{(1+i_{sl})}\right)} + \frac{\chi_l^l}{(1+i_{sl})^l} + \frac{\rho_l \cdot b \cdot (1+i) \cdot \left(1 - \frac{\chi_l^l}{(1+i_{sl})^l}\right)}{(1+i_{sl}) \cdot \left(1 - \frac{\chi_l}{(1+i_{sl})}\right)} - 1 \tag{4.33}$$

Reformulation of the first and third summands gives:

$$\lambda = \frac{i \cdot \chi_l \cdot \left(1 - \frac{\chi_l^l}{(1+i_{sl})^l}\right)}{(1+i_{sl} - \chi_l)} + \frac{\chi_l^l}{(1+i_{sl})^l} + \frac{\rho_l \cdot b \cdot (1+i) \cdot \left(1 - \frac{\chi_l^l}{(1+i_{sl})^l}\right)}{(1+i_{sl} - \chi_l)} - 1 \tag{4.34}$$

Giving them a common denominator results in:

$$\lambda = \frac{i \cdot \chi_l \cdot (1+i_{sl})^l \cdot \left(1 - \frac{\chi_l^l}{(1+i_{sl})^l}\right) + \chi_l^l \cdot (1+i_{sl} - \chi_l)}{(1+i_{sl} - \chi_l) \cdot (1+i_{sl})^l} \tag{4.35}$$

$$+ \frac{\rho_l \cdot b \cdot (1+i) \cdot (1+i_{sl})^l \cdot \left(1 - \frac{\chi_l^l}{(1+i_{sl})^l}\right) - (1+i_{sl} - \chi_l) \cdot (1+i_{sl})^l}{(1+i_{sl} - \chi_l) \cdot (1+i_{sl})^l}$$

Multiplying them out in the numerator results in:

$$\lambda = \frac{i \cdot \chi_l \cdot \left[(1 + i_{sl}^l) - \chi_l^l\right] + \chi_l^l \cdot (1 + i_{sl} - \chi_l)}{(1 + i_{sl} - \chi_l) \cdot (1 + i_{sl})^l}$$
$$+ \frac{\rho_l \cdot b \cdot (1 + i) \cdot \left[(1 + i_{sl}^l) - \chi_l^l\right] - (1 + i_{sl} - \chi_l) \cdot (1 + i_{sl})^l}{(1 + i_{sl} - \chi_l) \cdot (1 + i_{sl})^l} \tag{4.36}$$

Taking $(1 + i_{sl})^l$ and χ_l^l out of brackets gives:

$$\lambda = \frac{(1 + i_{sl})^l \cdot (i \cdot \chi_l + \rho_l \cdot b \cdot (1 + i) - 1 - i_{sl} + \chi_l)}{(1 + i_{sl} - \chi_l) \cdot (1 + i_{sl})^l}$$
$$+ \frac{\chi_l^l \cdot (1 + i_{sl} - \chi_l - i \cdot \chi_l - \rho_l \cdot b \cdot (1 + i))}{(1 + i_{sl} - \chi_l) \cdot (1 + i_{sl})^l} \tag{4.37}$$

The two right-hand brackets in the summands of the numerator are identical up to the reversed plus/minus sign, and may thus be taken out of brackets. In addition, other terms in these brackets may be put together, so that the following conclusion emerges:

$$\lambda = \frac{\left[(1 + i_{sl}^l) - \chi_l^l\right] \cdot \left[(1 + i) \cdot (\rho_l \cdot b + \chi_l) - (i_{sl} + 1)\right]}{(1 + i_{sl})^l \cdot (1 + i_{sl} - \chi_l)} \tag{4.38}$$

According to equation (4.32), − is the valuation correction in percentage terms in relation to the nominal value of the loan.

Appendix 6: Chapter 5 — Derivations

SECTION 5.2 DERIVATION

First of all equation (5.10) should be simplified for y. By applying the approximation formula [DMK/DPK92, S. 50]:

$$(1+x)^a \approx 1 + ax \tag{5.12}$$

can be written:

$$y \approx \frac{1 - n\rho_a - \sum_{k=1}^{n} \Delta\rho_k}{(1+i_s)^n} \tag{5.13}$$

The summand in the numerator is by definition equal to zero, as what we are concerned with here is the total of the deviations from the mean:

$$\sum_{k=1}^{n} \Delta\rho_k = 0 \tag{5.14}$$

So one obtains:

$$y \approx \frac{1 + n\rho_a}{(1+i_s)^n} \tag{5.15}$$

Renewed application of the approximation equation (5.12) in the numerator of formula (5.15) leads to:

$$y \approx \left(\frac{1 - \rho_a}{1 + i_s}\right)^n \tag{5.16}$$

On the assumption that it is, by way of approximation, permissible to use this approximate solution also for only j periods instead of for all n periods, equation (5.9) can be written as follows:

$$x \approx \sum_{j=1}^{n} \left(\frac{1 - \rho_a}{1 + i_s} \right)^{j} \qquad (5.17)$$

Here it is presupposed that for all values of j

$$\sum_{k=1}^{j} \Delta \rho_k \approx 0 \qquad (5.18)$$

applies with sufficient precision.

The sum in equation (5.17) is a geometric sequence with:

$$a_1 = \rho = \frac{1 - \rho_a}{1 + i_s} \qquad (5.19)$$

This leads to the following result:

$$x \approx \frac{\rho \cdot (1 - \rho^n)}{1 - \rho} \qquad (5.20)$$

By use of the substitution (5.19) equation (5.16) can be written as follows:

$$y \approx \rho^n \qquad (5.21)$$

By analogy with equation (5.17), equation (5.11) can, by way of approximation, be written as follows:

$$z \approx \sum_{j=1}^{n} \frac{(\rho_a + \Delta \rho_j) \cdot (1 - \rho_a)^{j-1}}{(1 + i_s)^j} = \sum_{j=1}^{n} \frac{(\rho_a + \Delta \rho_j)}{(1 - \rho_a)} \cdot \left(\frac{1 - \rho_a}{1 + i_s} \right)^{j} \qquad (5.22)$$

On the assumption that $\Delta \rho_j$ may, when adding up, be ignored — also by way of approximation — and by using equations (5.17) and (5.19) equation (5.22) can be written as follows:

$$z \approx \frac{\rho_a}{1 - \rho_a} \cdot \frac{\rho \cdot (1 - \rho^n)}{1 - \rho} \qquad (5.23)$$

The insertion of equations (5.20), (5.21) and (5.23) into equation (5.6) results in:

$$i \approx \frac{1 - \rho^n - \frac{b \cdot \rho_a \cdot \rho \cdot (1 - \rho^n)}{(1 - \rho_a) \cdot (1 - \rho)}}{\frac{\rho \cdot (1 - \rho^n)}{(1 - \rho)} + \frac{\rho \cdot (1 - \rho^n)}{(1 - \rho_a) \cdot (1 - \rho)}} \qquad (5.24)$$

Reduction by $(1 - \rho^n)$ and extension by $(1 - \rho)$ results in:

$$i \approx \frac{1 - \rho - \frac{b \cdot \rho_a \cdot \rho}{(1 - \rho_a)}}{\rho + \frac{b \cdot \rho_a \cdot \rho}{(1 - \rho_a)}} = \frac{1 - \rho \cdot \left(1 + \frac{b \cdot \rho_a}{1 - \rho_a} \right)}{\rho \cdot \left(1 + \frac{b \cdot \rho_a}{1 - \rho_a} \right)} \qquad (5.25)$$

Reverse substitution gives:

$$i \approx \frac{1 - \left(\frac{1-\rho_a}{1+i_s}\right) \cdot \left(1 + \frac{b \cdot \rho_a}{1-\rho_a}\right)}{\left(\frac{1-\rho_a}{1+i_s}\right) \cdot \left(1 + \frac{b \cdot \rho_a}{1-\rho_a}\right)} \tag{5.26}$$

Multiplying out gives:

$$i \approx \frac{1 - \frac{1-\rho_a + b \cdot \rho_a}{(1+i_s)}}{\frac{1-\rho_a + b \cdot \rho_a}{(1+i_s)}} \tag{5.27}$$

Extension by $(1 + i_s)$ and taking ρ_a out of brackets gives:

$$i \approx \frac{1 + i_s - 1 + \rho_a \cdot (1 - b)}{1 - \rho_a \cdot (1 - b)} = \frac{i_s + \rho_a \cdot (1 - b)}{1 - \rho_a \cdot (1 - b)} \tag{5.28}$$

$$i \approx \frac{i_s + \rho_a^*}{1 - \rho_a^*} \tag{5.29}$$

Comparison with equation (4.49) reveals that this is identical to equation (5.29). In the case of the variable ρ_j, equation (4.49) may thus — by way of approximation — likewise be used, in that the average ρ_a replaces the constant ρ.

SECTION 5.4 DERIVATION

Equation (5.30) may now, owing to the symmetries, be summarised as follows:

$$L = \sum_{j=1}^{n} \frac{\left\{ \left[i \cdot L + \frac{b \cdot \rho_j \cdot (1+i)}{(1-\rho_j)} \cdot L \right] \cdot \left[1 - \frac{(j-1)}{n} \right] + \frac{L}{n} \right\} \cdot \prod_{k=1}^{j} (1 - \rho_k)}{(1+i_s)^j} \tag{5.31}$$

After abbreviation by L, only the curved brackets are reformulated at first:

$$\{""\} = \left[i + \frac{b \cdot \rho_j}{1 - \rho_j} + i \cdot \frac{b \cdot \rho_j}{1 - \rho_j} \right] \cdot \left[\frac{n - j + 1}{n} \right] + \frac{1}{n} \tag{5.32}$$

$$\{""\} = \frac{\left[i \cdot \left(1 + \frac{b \cdot \rho_j}{1 - \rho_j} \right) + \frac{b \cdot \rho_j}{(1 - b_j)} \right] \cdot [n - j + 1] + 1}{n} \tag{5.33}$$

$$\{""\} = \frac{i \cdot \left(1 + \frac{b \cdot \rho_j}{1 - \rho_j} \right) \cdot (n - j + 1) + \frac{b \cdot \rho_j \cdot (n-j+1)}{1 - \rho_j} + 1}{n} \tag{5.34}$$

$$\{""\} = \frac{i}{n} \cdot \left[\left(1 + \frac{b \cdot \rho_j}{1 - \rho_j} + \frac{b \cdot \rho_j}{(1 + \rho_j) \cdot i} \right) \cdot (n - j + 1) + \frac{1}{i} \right] \tag{5.35}$$

$$\{""\} = \frac{i}{n} \cdot \left[\left(1 + \left(\frac{b \cdot \rho_j}{1 - \rho_j} \right) \cdot \left(1 + \frac{1}{i} \right) \right) \cdot (n - j + 1) + \frac{1}{i} \right] \tag{5.36}$$

Inserted into equation (5.30) abbreviated by L, and reformulated results in:

$$\frac{n}{i} = \sum_{j=1}^{n} \frac{\left[\left(1 + \left(\frac{b \cdot \rho_j}{1 - \rho_j}\right) \cdot \left(1 + \frac{1}{i}\right)\right) \cdot (n - j + 1) + \frac{1}{i}\right] \cdot \prod_{k=1}^{j}(1 - \rho_k)}{(1 + i_s)^j} \tag{5.37}$$

and transposed into:

$$i = \frac{n}{\displaystyle\sum_{j=1}^{n} \frac{\left[\left(1 + \left(\frac{b \cdot \rho_j}{1 - \rho_j}\right) \cdot \left(1 + \frac{1}{i}\right)\right) \cdot (n - j + 1) + \frac{1}{i}\right] \cdot \prod_{k=1}^{j}(1 - \rho_k)}{(1 + i_s)^j}} \tag{5.38}$$

Bibliography

ALT89   Altman, E. I.: Measuring Corporate Bond Mortality and Performance; in: *Journal of Finance*, **44**; 1989.

ALTM77   Altmann, E. I.; Haldeman, R. G.; Narayana, P.: Zeta Analysis: a New Model to Identify Bankrupty Risk of Corporations; in: *Journal of Banking and Finance*, June 1977, 29–54.

AUCK94   Auckenthaler, Christoph: *Finanzmathematische Grundlagen des Investment Banking*; Bern, Stuttgart, Wien 1994.

BCBS99   Basle Committee on Banking Supervision: *Credit Risk Modelling: Current Practices and Applications*; Basel 1999 (http://www.bis.org/wnew.htm).

BCCH97   Bakshi, Gurdip; Cao, Charles; Cen, Zhiwu: Empirical Performance of Alternative Option Pricing Models; in: *Journal of Finance*, **52** (2), December 1997.

BEDE97   Berger, Allen N.; DeYoung, Robert: Problem Loans and Cost Efficiency in Commercial Banks; in: *Journal of Banking & Finance*, **21**; 1997.

BLSC73   Black, Fischer; Scholes, Myron: The Pricing of Options and Corporate Liabilities; in: *Journal of Political Economy*; May–June 1973.

BOES96   Boeschenstein, Roland: Der Firmenkunde will mehr; in: *Handelszeitung Nr. 38*, 19.09.1996; Zürich 1996.

BOHL92   Bohley, Peter: *Statistik, Einführendes Lehrbuch für Wirtschafts- und Sozialwissenschaftler, 5.Auflage*; München, Wien, Oldenburg 1992.

BRAK91   Brakensiek, Thomas: *Die Kalkulation und Steuerung von Ausfallrisiken im Kreditgeschäft der Banken*; Frankfurt am Main 1991.

BRMY96   Brealey, Richard A.; Myers, Stewart C.: *Principles of Corporate Finance*; fifth edition; New York 1996.

BRUN94   Brunner, Christoph: *Bankübernahmen in der Schweiz*; Bern, Stuttgart, Wien 1994.

BRVA97   Briys, Eric; Varenne de, François: Valuing Risky Fixed Rate Debt: An Extension; in: *Journal of Financial and Quantitative Analysis*, **32** (2); June 1997.

BÜEV   Büschgen, Hans E.; Everling, Oliver *(Herausgeber): Handbuch Rating*; Wiesbaden 1996.

CAFA92   Carlson, John H.; Fabozzi, Frank J.: *The Trading and Securitization of Senior Bank Loans*; Chicago, Cambridge 1992.

CAOU98   Caouette, J. B.; Altmann, E. I.; Narayana, P.: *Managing Credit Risk: the Next Great Financial Challenge*; New York 1998.

CART98   Carty, Lea V.: Credit Risk and Credit Quality Correlation: What Can We Measure?; in: *Journal of Lending & Credit Risk Managment*; February 1998.

CHO98   Cho, Myeong-Hyeon: Ownership Structure, Investment, and Corporate Value: an Empirical Analysis; in: *Journal of Financial Economics*, **47** (1), January 1998, S. 103–121.

CHRI97   Chriss, Neil A.: *Black–Scholes and Beyond—Option Pricing Models*; Chicago/ London/Singapore 1997.

COME91   Cooper, I.; Mello, A.: The Default Risk of Swaps; in: *Journal of Finance*, **46**; 1991.

COPI01   Cossin, D.; Pirotte, H.: *Advanced Credit Risk Analysis*; Chichester 2001.

CORU85   Cox, John C.; Rubinstein, Mark: *Options Markets*; Englewood Cliffs 1985.

CPSH98   Carey, Mark; Part, Mitch; Sharp, Stevan A: Does Corporate Lending by Banks and Finance Companies Differ? Evidence on Specialization in Private Debt Contracting; in: *Journal of Finance*, **53**, June 1998 (http://www.cob.ohio-state.edn/htbin/htimage/~fin/journal/jf.conf? 94,154).

DICH98   Dicher, Ilia D.: Is the Risk of Bankruptcy a Systematic Risk?; in: *Journal of Finance*, **53**, June 1998 (http://www.cob.ohio-state.edn/htbin/htimage/~fin/journal/jf.conf?94,154).

DMK/DPK92   Deutschschweizerische Mathematikkommission; Deutschschweizerische Physikkommission: *Formeln und Tafeln Mathematik — Physik, 5. Auflage*; Zürich 1992.

DOSA97   Domowitz, la; Sartain, Robert L.: Determinants of the Consumer Bankruptcy Decision; in: *Journal of Finance*, forthcoming, http://www.cob.ohiostate-edu/htbin/htimage/~fin/journal/jf.conf?94,154.

DRZI98   Drzik, John: The Seven Stages of Risk Management; in: *Journal of Lending and Credit Risk Managment*; February 1998.

DUFF95a   Duffee, G. R.: On Measuring Credit Risks of Derivative Instruments; in: *Working Paper*, Federal Reserve Board, February 1995.

DUFF95b   Duffee, G. R.: On Variation of Default Risk with Treasury Yields; in: *Working Paper*, Federal Reserve Board, January 1995.

FHSS94   Flesaker, Bjorn; Hughston, Lune; Schreiber, Laurence; Sprung, Lloyd; Taking all the Credit; in: *Risk*, **7** (9) September 1994.

FRRM97   Fabozzi, Frank J.; Ramsey, Chuck; Ramirez, Frank R.; Marz, Michael: *The Handbook of Nonagency Mortgage-Backed Securities*; New Hope PA 1997.

FRSK97   Fooladi, Iraj J.; Roberts, Gordon S.; Shinner Frank: Duration for Bonds with Default Risk; in: *Journal of Banking & Finance*, **21**, 1997.

GAST92   Gastineau, Gary L.: *Dictionary of Financial Risk Management*; Chicago, Cambridge 1992.

GEJO84   Geske, Robert; Johnson, H. E.: The Valuation of Corporate Liabilities as Compound Options: A Correction; in: *Journal of Financial and Quantitative Analysis*, **19**, 1984.

GEKR   Gerdsmeier, Stefan; Krob Bernhard: Kundenindividuelle Bewertung des Ausfallrisikos mit dem Optionspreismodell; in: *Strategisches Bankcontrolling — Eine neue Herausforderung*; Publikation der DG Bank, Frankfurt am Main.

GESK74   Geske, Robert: The Valuation of Corporate Liabilities as Compound Options; in: *Journal of Financial and Quantitative Analysis*, **19**, 1984.

GLAN94   Glantz, Morton: *Loan Risk Management*; Chicago, Cambridge 1994.

GREN96   Grenadier, Steven R.: Leasing and Credit Risk; in: *Journal of Financial Economics*, **42** (3); November 1996.

HALB94   Halbherr, Philipp: Neuere theoretische Grundlagen zur Fundierung eines modernen Kreditmanagements; in: *Informations- und Arbeitstagung des Instituts für schweizerisches Bankwesen der Universität Zürich*; Zürich 1994.

HENN94   Henninger, Ute: *Branchenrisikoeinschätzung im Rahmen der Bonitätsbeurteilung von kommerziellen Kreditkunden*; Bern, Stuttgart, Wien 1994.

HOF95   Hof, Michael: Kreditderivate — Aktive Steuerung von Kreditrisiken; Vortrag am 14.09.1995 im Rahmen der IIR-Fachkonferenz "Kreditmanagement"; Publikation der DG Bank, Frankfurt am Main.

HOSI84   Ho, Thomas S. Y.; Singer, Ronald F.: The Value of Corporate Debt with a Sinking-Fund Provision; in: *Journal of Business*, **57**; 1984.

HULL97   Hull, John C.: *Options, Futures, and Other Derivatives*, third edition; Upper Saddle River 1997.

HÜRL93   Hürlimann, Werner: Risiko — aus morphologischer Sicht; in: *io Management Zeitschrift*, **62**; Zürich 1993.

HUWH92   Hull, J.; White A.: *The Price of Default*; in: *Risk*, September; 1992.

HUWH95   Hull, J.; White A.: The Impact of Default Risk on the Prices of Options and other Derivative Securities; in: *Journal of Banking and Finance*, **19** (May); 1995.

HSIA81   Hsia, Chi-Cheng: Optiomal Debt of a Firm: An Option Pricing Approach; in: *Journal of Financial Research*, **4**; 1981.

JATU95   Jarrow, R. A.: Turnbull, S. M.: Pricing Options on Derivative Securities Subject to Credit Risk; in: *Journal of Finance*, **50**; 1995.

JOST87   Johnson, H.; Stulz, R.: The Pricing of Options under Default Risk; in: *Journal of Finance*, **42**; 1987.

KAEL98   Kaelhofer, Stephen: Portfolio Management of Default Risk; in: http://www.kmv.com; 1998.

KARO93   Karolyi, Andrew G.: A Bayesian Approach to Modeling Stock Retrun Volatility for Option Valuation; in: *Journal of Financial and Quantitative Analysis*, **28** (4), December 1993.

KILG94   Kilgus, Ernst. *Strategisches Bank-Management*, Bern, Stuttgart, Wien 1994.

KNAB95   Knabenhans, Walter: Die Transparenz im Markt muss erhöht werden — Über die Zukunft, Chancen und Risiken des Derivativmarktes; in: *Finanz und Wirtschaft Nr. 18*, 04.03.1005; Zürich 1995.

KREY91   Kreyszig, Erwin: *Statistische Methoden und ihre Anwendung*, 7. Auflage; Göttingen 1991.

KRRO92   Kremer, Joseph W.; Roenfeldt, Rodney L.: Warrant Pricing: Jump-Diffusion vs. Black–Scholes; in: *Journal of Financial and Quantitative Analysis*, **28** (2), June 1992.

LEE81   Lee, C. Jerons: The Pricing of Corporate Debt: A Note; in: *Journal of Finance*, 36, 1981.

MANZ98   Manz, Felix: *Prozessorientiertes Kreditmanagement*; Bern, Stuttgart, Wien 1998.

MASU81   Mason, Scott P.; Sudipto, Bhattacharya: Risky Debt, Jump Processes, and Safety Covenants; in: *Journal of Financial Economics*, **9**, 1981.

MEIE96   Meier, Christian: *Lehren aus Verlusten im Kreditgeschäft Schweiz*; bern, Stuttgart, Wien 1996.

MERT73   Merton, R. C.: Theory of Rational Option Pricing; in: *Bell Journal of Economics and Management Science*, **4**, Frühling 1973.

MERT74   Merton, R. C.: On the Pricing of Corporate Debt: the Risk Structure of Interest Rates; in: *Journal of Finance*, **2**, 1974.

MOOD90   Moody's Investors Service: *Einführung Credit-Ratings am Kapitalmarkt*; Frankfurt, London, New York, Paris, San Francisco, Sydney, Tokyo 1990.

MÜLL90   Müller, Jörg: *Branchenkennzahlen zur Bonitätsbeurteilng von Klein- und Mittelunternehmungen — Eine empirische Studie anhand von Zahlenmaterial der SKA*; bankinterne Studie der SKA; Zürich 1990.

NATE94   Natenberg, Sheldon: *Option Volatility and Pricing*; Chicago, Cambridge 1994.

NEWT93   Newton, Brian: *Modeling Credit Risk*; New York 1993.

NZZ96   – *Acra statt Abracadabra, Das neue Risikosystem des Schweizerischen Bankvereins; Neue Zürcher Zeitung*, Nr. 218, Seite 29; Zürich 1996.
         – *Altlasten-Beseitigung bei der CS Holding; Neue Zürcher Zeitung*, Nr. 298, page 19; Zürich 1996.

PASS94   Passardi, Adriano: *Bank-Management und Bank-Kostenrechnung*; Bern, Stuttgart, Wien 1994.

RÄSS93   Räss, Hugo E.: *Die Resrukturierung von Unternehmen aus der Sicht der Kreditgebenden Bank*; Bern, Stuttgart, Wien 1993.

RITR98   Ritchken, Peter; Trevor, Rob: Pricing Options Under Generalized GARCH and Stochastic Volatility Process; in: *Journal of Finance*, forthcoming, http://www.cob.ohio-state.edu/htbin/htimage/˜fin/journal/jf.conf?94,154.

RSSO93   Reswick, Bruce G.; Sheikh, Aamir M.; Song, Yo-Shin: Time Varying Volatilities and Calculation of the Weighted Implied Standard Deviation; in: *Journal of Financial and Quantitative Analysis*, **28** (3); September 1993.

SAVE96   Savelberg, Albert H.: Risikomanagement mit Kreditderivaten; in: *Die Bank*, **6**, 1996.

SCMÜ98   Scholl, Martin; Müller, Roger: Risikogerechte Preise; in: *Schweizer Bank*; **1**; 1998.

SCHW82   Schwartz, Eduardo S: The Pricing of Commodity-Linked Bonds; in: *Journal of Finance*, **37**; 1982.

SDHJ97   Scott Docking, Diane; Hirschey, Mark; Jones Elaine: Information and Contragiven Effects of Bank Loan–Loss Reserve Announcements; in: *Journal of Financial Economics*, **43**; 1997.

SMIT76   Smith, Clifford W. Jr.: Option Pricing; in: *Journal of Financial Economics*, **3**; 1976.

SWDI92   Swidler, Steve; Diltz, David J.: Implied Volatilities and Transaction Costs; in: *Journal of Financial and Quantitative Analysis*, **27** (3); September 1992.

TRTU96   Tripi, R.; Turban, E.,: Neural Networks in Finance and Investing; in: http://www.sigma-research.com/bookshelf/rtbookn2.thm.

VASI84   Vasicek; Oldrich A.: Credit Valuation; in: http://www.kmv.com; 1984.

VIZA96   Vintschger von, R.; Zaker, S.: Kreditrisiken sind gefährlicher als Marktrisiken; in: *Finanz und Wirtschaft*, 21.09.1996; Zürich 1996.

VOLK93   Volkart, Rudolf: *Beiträge zur Theorie und Praxis des Finanzmanagements*, 5. erweiterte Auflage; Zürich 1993.

VOLK98/1 Volkart, Rudolf: Optionswertbildung und Optionspreistheorie — Versuch einer integrierten 'didaktischen' Darstellung; in: *Working Paper Serie* (Institut für schweizerisches Bankwesen der Universität Zürich), Zürich 1998.

VOLK98/2 Volkart, Rudolf: Optionstheoretische Überlegungen zur Kapitalstrukturgestaltung und zur Kreditfinanzierung; in: *Working Paper Serie* (Institut für schweizerisches Bankwesen der Universität Zürich), Zürich 1998.

VOLK99   Volkart, Rudolf: Optionstheoretische Analyse von Fremdkapitalkontrakten und alternative Credit Risk Spread-Bestimmungen — eine integriete Darstellung; in: *Working Paper Serie* (Institut für schweizerisches Bankwesen der Universität Zürich), Zürich 1999.

WONG97   Wong, Kit Pang: On the Determinants of Bank Interest Margins under Credit and Interest Rate Risks; in: *Journal of Banking and Finance*, **21**; 1997.

ZELL83   Zellweger, Bruno: *Überwachung kommerzieller Bankkredite*; Bern, Stuttgart 1983.

ZIMM98   Zimmermann, Heinz: $C = S \times N(d_1) - X \cdot e^{-r.(T-t)} \times N(d_2)$; in: *Schweizer Bank*; 1998.

ZKB96   Zürcher Kantonalbank: *Immobilienmarkt Zürich; Eigenverlag*; Zürich 1996.

Index

Compiled by Annette Musker